Ena~...

By the first paragraph of the introduction, Andrea had me hooked. Reading *Freaking Out to Flying Free* is like having a long, uplifting conversation with a very wise friend who offers compassion, understanding, simple wisdom, and great advice. This book helped me find freedom from the structured rigidity of the "rules trump relationships" mindset that held me bound for far too long.

—Alan Goff, Results Consultant, Achievement Accelerator, Goals Guru, Leadership & Mental-Toughness Success Coach, Professional Speaker

Freaking Out to Flying Free is a very personal account of Andrea's journey to freedom. Key spiritual principles, drawn from the wells of challenge and suffering, are presented with passion and clarity. Practical help and insight are woven into the pages of this book and those who long to enjoy the freedom Christ offers will benefit from reading it.

—Lyndon Wall, Refresh Ministries

I've been blessed to know Andrea for quite a few months now, and I can say she is the "real deal." She lives out her faith in a most beautiful way. I had the privilege of reading in-depth and more than one time, the manuscript for *Freaking Out to Flying Free*, and let me say, it is well done! In it, Andrea openly shares her journey to freedom, often learned through the hard things in life. She doesn't share with a "look how far I've come" attitude; rather it is with a deep desire for each one of us to experience that same freedom. She lays out the principles God taught her in such a way that those who are just beginning the journey toward freedom and those who are

.

well on their way will all benefit. If you desire to live a life of freedom, or even if you currently are, this is a must read.

—Lori Heitrich, Author: *Losing Lance: One Life Matters,* Grief Recovery Specialist

I have watched Andrea walk out the principles that she shares in this valuable book. Having gotten to know her over the last several months, I know that she does indeed rely on her Father God as her All-Sufficient Source. I pray that you, too, may find freedom in Jesus to fly free.

—Kendra Madsen, Executive Director, Pregnancy Care Centre Grande Prairie

I heartily recommend this book to all who are seeking God and wanting His abundant life.

—Gwen Hagerman, Keynote Speaker

Freaking Out to Flying Free is an honest and candid account of the author's personal struggles and keys to victory that she has discovered along her life's path. I appreciate Andrea's openness to share from her own weaknesses and vulnerability as she guides the reader into a vital relationship with God and to principles found in His Word that bring true freedom to our lives. I am confident that as you read this book you will find true help to overcome and become a winner in every area of your life.

—Victoria Lindahl*, Author: *Significance—One Life Can Make a Difference*

*The Author's Name has been changed for security reasons.

If you feel uneasy but can't put your finger on why, *Freaking Out to Flying Free* is for you! I wouldn't admit I was freaking out before. I was trying to hold it all together. Andrea allowed me to find the freedom killers in my life and be set free! Are you ready to be set free? Read the book, get on a coaching call. Andrea Fehr is the woman of God you need in your life!

—Brenda Haire, Author: *Save the Butter Tubs!*
Discover Your Worth in a Disposable World

Andrea Fehr is the incredible author of the book *Freaking Out to Flying Free*. This step-by-step book is a refreshing work that takes everyday circumstances and brings the truth and the heart of our Savior into our everyday lives to show us how to have freedom in overcoming and to have abundant life. Andrea uses her incredible testimony throughout this book to show us how to walk into our own freedom and fly into our destiny. God's promises are lived out through Andrea's testimony, and from her experiences, she is able to minister freely, helping us to break bonds of fear and self-defeating habits, and to discover our own freedom through this exceptional book. It has been my honor to partner in prayer with Andrea and her dreams to launch this book and ministry, and to watch how God is unfolding Andrea's great destiny and purpose. Andrea unlocks our ability to ask questions, allowing us to discover our deepest desire to find freedom and purpose in the chaos of our circumstances. I highly recommend this work of discovery and freedom ministries!

—Kimberly Talmey, KAT-al-yst Coaching and
Counseling Services

Freaking Out
To
Flying Free

Dearest ████
You are the 1st ████
absolutely
live autographed any
book for. :)
Enjoy flying free.
♡ M

Freaking Out
To
Flying Free

Experience Freedom Amid
the Chaos of Life

ANDREA FEHR

Copyright 2018 by Andrea Fehr

All rights reserved. This book or any portion thereof may not be reproduced or used in any manner whatsoever without the express written permission of the publisher except for the use of brief quotes.

Published by Author Academy Elite
Author Academy Elite
PO Box 43
Powell, OH, 43065
Printed in the United States of America

Paperback: 978-1-64085-287-7

Hardback: 978-1-64085-288-4

Library of Congress Control Number: 2018941941

Unless otherwise noted, Scripture quotations are from the Holy Bible, English Standard Version, ESV, Copyright 2001, 2002, 2007 Text Edition, by Crossway Bibles, a publishing ministry of Good News Publishers. Used by permission of Good News Publishers. All rights reserved. The "ESV" and "English Standard Version" are registered trademarks of Good News Publishers. Use of either trademark requires the permission of Good News Publishers.

Scripture quotes marked NLT are taken from the Holy Bible, New Living Translation, Copyright 1996, 2004, 2007 by Tyndale House Foundation. Used by permission of Tyndale House Publishers, Inc., Carol Stream, Illinois 60188. All rights reserved.

Scripture quote marked The Message, Copyright 1993, 1994, 1995, 1996, 2000, 2001, 2002 by Eugene H. Peterson. Used by permission of NavPress. All rights reserved. Represented by Tyndale House Publishers, Inc.

Dedicated to my everyday Savior, who has led me every single step of the way. You alone are worthy of all praise and glory.

～ ～ ～

To my brother, Byron Jonathan Porritt.
The way you lived inspired me to pursue my dreams.

～ ～ ～

To my ever-supportive knight in shining armor,
Calvin Benjamin Fehr, and our wonderful children:
Alaythea, Benjamin, Michael, and Joshua.
You inspired me to obey God, even when the journey
was scary, long, and hard. I trust He will use
my book to set you free to fly.

～ ～ ～

To my fellow warriors who are sick of freaking out
and ready to fly free!

Contents

"The truth is there is only one freedom -- the holy freedom of Christ,
Whereby He freed us from sin, from evil, from the devil.
It binds us to God.
All other freedoms are illusory, false,
That is to say, they are all, in fact,
slavery."

~Justin Popovic

INTRODUCTION

Invitation

Invitation

The abundant life. Victorious living. Freedom in Christ. These words tormented me for a very long time. If I, a person of faith, was supposed to have abundant life, why was I not experiencing it? How did one actually live victoriously? What did freedom in Christ really mean, and if I had it, what would it look like?

I wrestled with the sinking feeling that I was missing out on something tremendous, something that was supposed to be mine but wasn't because I was living the Christian life wrong. I was hanging out with Jesus by attending church and having personal times of study and prayer with Him, but I still didn't feel like I was living the abundant life.

Why couldn't I experience freedom? What was I missing?

For my whole life, God has been using my deep longing for a victorious life to draw me to Himself. I wouldn't say it has been pretty, but it has been completely worth it. God has faithfully revealed to me that I am meant to experience His abundant life, to know and live the freedom and victory He created for me.

In the process of learning what abundant life really is and the application of it in my life, God nudged my heart to write this book. I began to be aware that the time to write was now. I wrestled with fears and doubts, but God was firm in imprinting the word "FREEDOM" on my heart and mind. So with trepidation, I have stepped out in faith, and God has repeatedly provided what I have needed for each and every page of this book.

Not only has He made clear the process He uses to bring freedom to my life, but He has also provided you, a soul longing to live abundantly, be victorious, and fly free amid the chaos of life. I am truly thankful for you and for our good God who has connected us.

God has transformed me from feeling constantly defeated in my life with Christ into being a woman who knows who she is, what she's here for, and where she's going -- a woman who lives the life of a victorious warrior, embracing her God-given ability to fly free amid the chaos of life.

Words like "free," "easy," "yoke," "rest," "abide," and "peace" aren't in the Bible just because they look and sound nice. They are there for us to walk in. They are gifts our loving Father provides for us for life down on this earth, in this fallen world where hard things happen.

Years ago, I was in a seminar where they talked about the book *The Prayer of Jabez*[1] by Bruce Wilkinson. My take-away was from the chapter that spoke of a huge room full of gifts. Someone inquired about whose gifts they were. The depressing response was that they were the gifts God's children were given but had never opened. I was deeply touched by that story and purposed in my heart to open every single gift God has for me.

We can't earn these gifts, but we do need to learn how to receive them. And we can -- at the feet of Jesus. In the book of Matthew, God promises He will give rest for our souls. He promises that once He has set us free from sin, we are free. And so, we are. It is up to us to accept the gifts He offers us.

Through the help of many authors, speakers, friends, and countless Holy Spirit encounters, I began to let God Almighty catch me with His presence, peace, and grace. He has transformed my heart and mind, truly bringing me to a walk of freedom that is radical and refreshing.

It's not just for me, though. It is for anyone willing to receive the gifts He died to give us. So, dear one who desires to fly free amid the chaos of life, get excited! In the next chapters you will learn how to discover what has been holding you back and how God has provided a way for you to fly free.

As I have wrestled with depression, chronic illness, and grief, I have personally tested the truths God teaches. I invite you to join me in opening the gift of freedom because no matter what we are facing, we can fly free in Him.

PART ONE

Investigate

CHAPTER 1

Remember When...

*"Just living is not enough... one must have
sunshine, freedom, and a little flower."*

Hans Christian Anderson

The blue swing set is occupied again. A little girl with two long brown braids is clutching the swing's ropes. Sheer joy and expectation radiate from her face as she begins propelling the swing back and forth, back and forth. Her legs pump at a peaceful pace, and as she soars, she leans back further and further. Higher and higher she goes, arms fully extended, legs nearly vertical in the air, eyes closed, face glowing, dimples showing, huge grin. She is flying.

Suddenly there is a thud. She feels pain, and tears flow. The girl's hands had left the ropes, causing her head to crash on the ground. Whether her hands slipped or in her ecstasy she simply forgot to keep holding on, we may never know. What we do know is this: The sequence is repeated until a voice with an unseen face calls out from the house, "Keep holding on!"

Does this story reflect your experience with victorious living and abundant life? It may seem as though you are soaring one minute, and then in the next, the reality of your struggles crashes you back down to earth. With a painful thud, you begin to believe that flying free amid the chaos of life is impossible.

Freedom: What is it? When can we have it? Would we recognize it? Who controls it?

Abundant life: What would that look like? Why are so few claiming to experience it? What exactly is flying free? Is it possible to experience while on earth or is it ever-elusive like it was for me...the girl on the swing?

All of us have asked some of these questions or we wouldn't be here today beginning this journey together. I'm so glad you've joined me and I believe you will be pleasantly surprised by what we learn. Before we move forward in our journey, let us first glimpse over our shoulders and look back. Can you remember the last time you felt free?

When was the last time you were overflowing with life and joy? When were you so deeply content, all you could do was sigh and grin? When was the last time your heart and mind were so at peace that when something came up and upset the schedule, system, project, or relationship, you simply paused, took a deep breath, and knew it would all work out? Take a minute, sip your hot beverage, and ponder these questions.

Can you conjure up a picture of what freedom looked like for you as a child, teen, or adult? What events surrounded that feeling of freedom? How long did the freedom last? What interrupted that moment, causing it to end?

Bear with me; these questions are paving the way for us to hone in on what freedom really is. Throughout this book, we will investigate how triggers attempt to rob us of our freedom. We will see hard evidence that proves there are freedom-killers out to get us, and we will realize that God has freedom-builders to face each killer. By investing in these freedom-builders, we will be able to skip the "thud" more often and instead fly. Before we do that, however, I'd like to invite you to enjoy these pictures of freedom with me:

Flying free is that moment you flew down the hill on your bike as a child full of joy, peace, and hopeful anticipation.

Flying free is the energy that consumes you, causing you to put everything into your project or recital piece, not for the outcome, but for the sheer pleasure of being able to be all in: body, mind, and soul.

Flying free is the ability to be at peace internally no matter what.

Through my first thirteen years of being a mom, I wrestled with chronic illness. Amid the suffering, I became ensnared in self-condemnation. It led me so far down the road of depression that I contemplated suicide. The path of internal bondage robbed me. Instead of simply enjoying who I am and what I could do, I would waste time and energy, consumed with what others may be thinking about me. God was at work in my mess, growing in me the desire for the freedom Jesus speaks of and lives out in the Bible.

Jesus was not stressed out while here on earth. Neither was He freaking out, wondering what others were thinking of Him. He wasn't kicking Himself for not doing this or that right. Quite the contrary, He exuded confidence and passion while facing those who opposed Him during His time here on earth.

From the age of 30, He moved in position from "the carpenter's son" to a sought-after teacher. In Mark 4, He spoke in His hometown and they were shocked to hear His confidence and clarity. After that, He began to invite individuals to join Him in His calling to present the good news to the country. They left their various occupations and followed Him. People don't leave behind their families and jobs to join a freaking out, fear-driven person. I suggest to you that Jesus emanated peace and purpose. In the book of John, we see that Jesus was abiding in His Father's love and obeying His every word, keenly aware of His presence each moment. He is our example of the abundant life.

We have never been invited to a stressed-out, panicked existence full of fear, worry, rage, and frustration. We have, however, been invited to be a part of God's plan - a plan that includes a relationship with Him that is so real and intimate, it affects our responses and attitudes when the hard things in life hit us. It's a call to a God-directed life, in which we connect with God the Father like Jesus did, through moment-by-moment reliance on Him.

Before you say, "I've heard all this before, and it hasn't helped me in my everyday chaos." Remember, friends, that when Jesus was resurrected and went up to Heaven, His very Spirit was sent to dwell within us. This is what enables us to live the abundant life full of peace and purpose, contentment and confidence. He told His followers in the book of John that it was better for them if He left so that the Holy Spirit would come be with them, teaching them.

Ahead we will discover what is holding us back from receiving this gift. We will become aware of God's solutions. As a result, we will be able to fly free, no matter what we are facing. I promise you the work will be worth it. If you are feeling resistance, acknowledge its presence, but don't let it lie to you any longer. We were created to live in freedom with our Creator, flying through the chaos of life with His confidence, joy, and purpose.

CHAPTER 2

Know Your M.O.

"For the law of the Spirit of life in Christ Jesus hath made me free from the law of sin and death."

Romans 8:2

The alarm goes off, slowly penetrating your consciousness. As your mind begins to process the sound, your heart responds with a feeling. What is that feeling usually? What is the first thought to follow the feeling?

My first thoughts in the morning run a gambit of anything from, "No, not another day," to, "Oh, I'm so tired," or on my favorite days, excitement and a desire to get going.

Maybe you can't remember having to set an alarm because you have living alarms. They wake you up throughout the night on any whim that is currently affecting them. In fact, it's a miracle to wake up on your own or to feel remotely awake when you are up. It is truly a wondrous event when you are finally able to creep out of bed to the kitchen for a cup of coffee in solitude.

The point of this exercise is for us to begin to discern our mode of operation, or M.O. Before I share the framework that enables us to fly, we need to recognize the triggers that have become our foundation for operation. Basically, we need to discover what isn't working. As we become aware of our triggers, we will be able to discern when to activate our freedom framework. Once we have developed this self-awareness and allowed ourselves to dream of living freely, then we will be in the perfect position to apply the freedom solutions God has for us.

Some of you may be rolling your eyes at this concept because you feel it is impossible to be aware of our M.O. It can be learned, my friend. I am convinced of this, and it is most definitely worth our while, so please hang in there with me. Here are some questions to get the self-awareness pumps primed:

What is motivating you this morning?

What is pushing you to read this book?

What is the fuel feeding your personal fire?

Why did this book interest you?

What would you like to see become different in your life?

How do you feel about your life?

How do you feel about the items on your "to do" list?

How do you feel about the activities in your schedule?

Why did you sign up for them?

What is your passion?

If you feel stumped by any of these questions, don't panic. That is ok; this is a learning process. It makes sense to feel overwhelmed at first, but press on. It will be worth it! Developing self-awareness is crucial for success in implementing the freedom framework.

To develop self-awareness, break down your day into chunks, such as morning, afternoon, and evening. Spend time thinking through what happened in your morning. Then grab a piece of paper or journal and write, "This morning I…" Jot down what you did and how it made you feel. It doesn't need to be fancy. Don't overthink this. Just do it.

Good job!

Next, what emotions do you experience when you see the plans for 12-6 pm? The same goes for the evening. When you consider 6-10 pm tonight, what thoughts and/or emotions surface?

I realize that each day of the week is different, but that is the beauty of doing this exercise, it doesn't matter what is happening in your day just jot down your reaction to it. Please don't let this be a four-hour process. Five to ten minutes should suffice. As you practice doing self-checks throughout your day, it becomes more natural, taking only moments to complete.

Here are some examples of what my self-checks looked like when I had four small children at home:

Morning:

I sit in my old, pink recliner, watching my beauty feed, dozing while hoping and praying we both can go back to sleep. I find myself worrying that someone will wake us up fully by being loud or needing me for something. A desperate need for sleep fogs my thoughts, leading me to "what ifs" and eventually to tears of pity and defeat.

My self-check would sound like this: What I was experienced this morning was exhaustion, worry, and sadness while feeding my baby.

Afternoon:

The kids are settled for their quiet time. I am so thankful to be horizontal, I let out a satisfied moan. Quickly I shush myself for fear that I will wake up the baby. I listen once more to be sure the older kids aren't too loud. All is well, so I snuggle in and surrender to the sweet floating sensation of sleep. BANG, BANG, BANG! I jolt upright, heart rate soaring, fury rising. BANG, BANG, BANG!

I snap to my senses and fly off the bed, opening the door savagely. I glare down into the solemn eyes of the invader and hear, "Mommy, our show is done. Can we watch one more?"

I work to reign in my frustration at the interruption. I feel relief that the baby is still asleep. I acknowledge how lovely it would be to have alone time and grant the invader his wish.

My self-check may sound like this:

When I think of the afternoon, I feel excited about a nap, then anxious about possible interruptions during nap time. I feel guilty about letting the kids watch TV again and frustrated that I don't feel more awake.

Evening:

I hear myself snip and snap at little ones who aren't trying to drive me crazy. I struggle to stay awake after supper and then fume when bed time doesn't get accomplished in record time. I remove myself from helping with bedtime routines and focus my ire on the kitchen clean-up. The kids are in bed and my husband wants to talk, but I feel exhausted and annoyed at every turn, so I tell him I need to go for a walk. I return to the house closer to peace than before and eventually connect with my husband. I feel ashamed of my inner angst earlier in the evening.

My self-check may sound like this:

Evenings are brutal! I am so tired and frustrated. I feel trapped. I'm failing in my reactions and responses.

As you read these examples you may have recognized similar words reoccurring: fatigue, fear, anxiety, pressure, guilt, and frustration. These emotions have been triggered by an event or thought, and how I respond to them becomes my mode of operation.

Triggers are a fact of life, and they are gifts from God, inviting us to further investigate why we are going into a specific M.O. It can be rather overwhelming to see what mode we have been operating out of, but it is necessary to discover this information. Through this investigation, we become more aware of which freedom-killers we are falling for. I've discovered three main triggers that lead me to modes of operation that ground me. By being aware of my main triggers, I can more easily recognize my responsibility to choose. Will I choose a freedom-killer or builder?

In the next part of the book, we will learn which freedom-killers we tend to lean toward and what solutions God provides. The purpose of this section is to simply become more aware of what our triggers are and where they can lead us.

There are numerous triggers and modes of operation. The participants in my Flying Free Coaching Group pointed out perfectionism, being overwhelmed, and lack of clarity as triggers. For me, the three that have hit with frequency are fatigue, fear, and internal pressure.

I have struggled with chronic fatigue syndrome for around 15 years, so I am intimately aware of how it affects each part of me. Fatigue has a way of making emotions very loud, to which I'm sure all who have worked with over-tired children can relate. Fatigue affects adults in similar ways. We just aren't usually honest enough to admit it. There is nothing wrong with being tired. Tiredness is part of being human. However, when we allow this trigger to be in charge, we have a problem.

When we allow fatigue to be what we operate out of, life gets rough for us and those around us. This I have learned first-hand. Our perspective is skewed when we are tired. Our emotions are loud and overpowering. Fatigue in charge will make demands that are self-serving and irrational. Fatigue itself is not wrong; it's a part of life on earth. Fatigue in charge is bondage. If fatigue is one of your triggers, rest assured in this: God taught me how to use it in a way that led me to fly free, and He can help you do this too.

Another trigger I often operated out of was fear. Fear-based reasoning has sabotaged my ability to fly more times than I care to count, like when my husband wanted us to move to an acreage, but I was terrified that mice would get into our house. Fear-based reasoning clips the wings of freedom, leaving us trapped in a cage of our own making.

In college I could often be heard saying, "I can't because I have so much work to do." This may have been true, or it could have been me hiding behind my fear that I must finish my assignments before the deadline because what if my computer dies and I need extra time, or what if I get sick and can't get it done in time?

A freedom-based response would have been, "That sounds like so much fun. Let me check if I can reschedule this homework for later this week." Fear-based motivation makes decisions to the exclusion of fun, risk-taking, and even divine appointments.

I once had an opportunity to chat with a friend who was struggling with deep depression. Because it was my bed time, I worried as I went, wondering if I would end up more physically depleted than I already was. Since I wrestled with chronic fatigue, that could mean having to stay in bed the next day because my legs would not be able to function. I am so thankful that I didn't let fear win, but I chose instead to trust that God would provide and went to be with my dear friend.

Fear will never give up anything it's offered, so I have had to learn to disallow it control. Becoming more aware of it has given me the edge I need to stop it in its tracks. We'll talk more about this later in the book.

Remember my self-check as a mom of small children? You can see in my words the pressure I felt when I let my kids watch more tv than I thought they should. Added to that was the frustration with myself for being snappy even though I could hardly see straight because of the exhaustion I was experiencing.

Internal pressure is the "should" voice we experience. It may sound something like this:

"I should be on that committee because everyone has to be on a committee at some point, right?"

"I should call so-and-so because I haven't in forever, and what is she going to think of me if I don't ask her about...?"

"I really should sit down and play with the kids. I think good moms do that. I really don't want to, and they are playing happily, but I should …"

Internal pressure puts handcuffs on our God-given right to choose our actions. Internal pressure pushes and squeezes us into submission, thereby clipping our wings.

As you run self-checks over the next few days, you may realize that your triggers are anger, hunger, or stress. It doesn't matter what they are; just become aware of them. This book is not about judging triggers or ourselves. Our purpose in this chapter is to simply acknowledge that we each have triggers and that some send us into freak-out mode faster than others.

Triggers help us recognize when we have a choice to make. We can then change direction and move from freaking out to implementing the freedom framework. I am so thrilled to share with you that each of my triggers have less holding power as I have grown in my awareness of them. I fly free by being aware of them and then choosing to cut them off as soon as they attempt to lead me toward freaking out.

Now it's your turn. Please take some time to work through the following questions. If you think, "I don't freak out that much. I don't need to develop awareness," please ignore that thought. By choosing to become more aware of your triggers, you are putting yourself into a position to receive all God has for you. You may be surprised. You may even realize that you are on the verge of freaking out more often than you thought. You will discover as you go through this process that you are able to teach it to those in your sphere of influence, impacting their lives in a profound way.

So set your timer for fifteen minutes if you need to, and work your way through these questions:

Did any of the triggers mentioned above resonate with you? If so, which ones?

Can you hear a bossy inner voice demanding more and more from you?

Is there a sense of shame or condemnation that keeps telling you that you are doing it all wrong?

Write down the top three triggers that lead you to freaking out the most often.

Maybe stress motivates you to action. Deadlines breathing down your neck help you execute the plan. The problem is that you are becoming a casualty as your body absorbs the stress and your adrenaline continues to run too high.

Perhaps anger is what pops up first for you when life throws you a curveball. How often have you felt angry today? In the last week?

We all respond to what happens in life. When triggers become something we acknowledge, we can then decide which mode of operation we will continue in. If we choose not to become aware of the triggers and modes of operation that lead to freaking out, they will continue robbing us of the life we were meant to live.

I'm so glad you are choosing to learn more with me. Get excited! In the next section we will discover the freedom-builders that will give you power over freaking out.

PART TWO

Invest

CHAPTER 3

My Source

*"Do not be afraid to be saints. Follow Jesus Christ who is the
source of freedom and light. Be open to the Lord so that
He may lighten all your ways."*

-Pope John Paul II-

I was introduced to the Source of my freedom and my victory
as a youngster. At the age of four, I received His friendship.
I remember that moment in detail. My friend and I were at
Kids Club in a church basement. We had played, *The Farmer
in the Dell,* in the church yard earlier. It had been so much
fun. Now it was time for the Bible story. The speaker had
created a car and road from paper and shared how we each had
a choice. The narrow road was the best way. It led to Heaven,
but few chose it because it was also a hard road.

I heard how Jesus wants us to live with Him now and in
Heaven after we die, how He came to earth to pay the price
for our rebellious choices against Him called sin. If I believed
I had sinned but that He loved me enough to die for my sin,

then I could walk with Him on the narrow road that would one day lead me to Heaven.

When the teacher asked who wanted to live life God's way, I raised my hand. I wanted to go to Heaven, and my heart was nudging me to accept this invitation. I even raised my best friend's hand because I really wanted her in Heaven with me when we died!

Later, I knelt by a bench with someone and thanked Jesus for paying the price for my sin so that I could be forgiven and go to Heaven when I die. I remember a window above me as I prayed. I looked up and there was a bright light streaming through the window. It was a joyful and soul-soothing experience.

The sad part of the story is this: Somewhere in my meeting Jesus, the concept that He would walk each moment fully with me did not connect with my heart. You'll hear more about the effect that had on me in the next couple of chapters.

I've been friends with God the Almighty Creator and Sustainer of Life, for over three decades now. Each year I grow to love and trust Him more. I have come to deeply believe that He fully knows me and daily desires to journey with me. He is committed to loving me; to forgiving my daily mess-ups; and to teaching, training, and leading me. My Source is the real deal, never leaving me high and dry. At times in my life, I felt ignored by Him. When I've asked Him about those times, He has comforted my heart, opening my eyes to how He was there.

I can hear hurt souls saying, "That's nice for you, but that is not my experience." I am so sorry for the hurt you've been through as a child and/or adult. It is dreadful that you were wounded by those who were to love and protect you but broke your trust.

If you are struggling to believe that God can be your sustainable, unchanging Source, you are not alone. We all wrestle with belief - every single day. And life is hard. We will have to decide if we'll go through life with or without God. The One who made and saved us wants a daily relationship with us. What have we got to lose if we accept His invitation?

Although I have been friends with Jesus for a long time, I have wrestled with believing He will care for me daily. However, as I look over the last three decades, I can see His faithful hand all over my life. For that, I am so thankful. Without Jesus as my Source, it would be impossible for me to fly free.

Maybe you have Jesus as your Source, or you thought you did, but you still wrestle with flying free. That's ok. It's totally normal. It is my prayer that through this book you will be able to sort this out and become a frequent flyer.

Life has a way of opening our eyes to our needs and weaknesses. I heard a lady once share her story of becoming a follower of Jesus. She had become a Christian later in life, and she stated, "Life is hard. You can do it with God or without Him." Personally, I thought I was doing life with God because I had accepted His gift of forgiveness, but I hadn't really understood that He is my everyday Savior who desires for me to depend on Him each day.

My Source truly became my Source after I was married.

I had dabbled in experiencing weakness on a drama tour team. I still remember: I believe it was our first away from home performance. As I stood on stage waiting for my cue to enter the drama, a teammate looked at me and asked, "Are you nervous?"

"Oh, yeah!" I whispered back.

"Good," he said.

"What?" I questioned in shock.

"When we are weak, He is strong." he said. And with that the drama began.

I wanted to experience my Source as all-powerful, but at the cost of me experiencing major weakness...well, that didn't sound like much fun. And it wasn't, but it's been worth it to come to believe that it's normal for me to be weak, and wise for me to not fight it, but to instead lean on God, inviting His strength into my life.

I didn't know it at the time, but by the end of our second year of marriage, I was embarking on serious "I am weak, but He is not" boot camp. It was a reality check on how much I was truly allowing God to be my Source.

My energy levels had dropped noticeably. I would wake up exhausted, go to work, then come home and nap. Often, I would wake up and then not be able to get ready for work due to a fatigue so deep, it would literally affect my ability to walk. Because of that, I used up my entire sick leave at my job as an educational assistant. This was the beginning of a long, hard road of chronic illness.

Fast-forward fourteen years, where as a mother of four beautiful children, I remember sitting on a stool in our kitchen wanting to participate fully in the beehive of activity. However, the very effort of sitting on my stool was all I could manage. I remember asking my husband with tears in my eyes, "Can you see God in my weakness?"

The weakness was so deep, so strong, so wide. I felt utterly trapped in its clutches. I remember one day being in bed feeling unable to lift the sheet, let alone drag myself out of bed. It has been through this season of physical weakness that I have discovered how God alone is my Source and that He is the only one I can fully count on.

When the fatigue didn't attack my legs, it would attack my lungs. I felt like I was being choked. I'd gasp for breath as all strength left my body. This would happen at random times. My dear husband, Calvin, has carried me out of events. My dad has run across town to be with our small children during an attack. Friends have witnessed my fatigue attacks and grieved with me in my weakness. I have battled, wrestled, panicked, and prayed my way through these attacks.

As time went on and no answers, solutions, or healing were found, my ability to will the attacks to stop began to die. My belief that the doctors could help also began to die. I'd hope and wonder and then again be devastated that there was no answer for me. It was brutal on me and on Calvin. Slowly God used this painful process to help me begin to believe that He alone could be my strength, my hope, my rest, my joy, my everything.

We live in a broken world, but when God created the world, it was good. You can check out the book of Genesis in the Bible to read more about it. He created man and woman, and they had a deep and beautiful relationship with Him. He did give them one rule because He wanted them to love Him and trust Him. They chose to break that rule, and in doing so, they introduced sin to every person thereafter. By sinning, they also broke their perfect relationship with God. They couldn't fix their relationship with God because of their sin, and neither can we. However, God loved us so very much that He sent His Son to pay the price for our sin through dying on the cross. He alone is perfect. Only He could pay the punishment for all. Jesus completed the punishment, then rose from the dead because none of the sins were His own. Now we can have a restored relationship with Him, but each one of us must choose. Will we walk with Him through life or not?

I know that we could argue that it wasn't our fault. The first man and woman sinned, not us. But if we are truly honest with ourselves, we know that often we have felt that our way is better than God's. It's about perspective. Am I the created truly believing that I know more than Almighty God the Creator? Will I really try to live as though I know more than the All-Knowing One?

Whether you believe God to be your Creator or not, would you still be willing to pause for a minute and ask yourselves these questions:

When did you last feel free, and what was the source of that freedom?

Is that source sustainable?

Is that source subject to change?

Does that source have your best interest in mind?

Will that source be helpful even when you have blown it big time?

Is that source a being that can respond to you?

Does that source faithfully give you all you need to fly free amid life's chaos and brokenness?

Is your source leading you to life or death?

Would you recommend your source to your loved ones?

So, my dear readers, I don't know what is fueling your desire to break your pattern of freaking out. Part of it for me is that the freak-out pattern is exhausting and so opposite of how I want to live and model life for my loved ones. Would you acknowledge with me that no matter how determined, organized, and educated we are, there are still many times daily that we are in over our heads? Would you agree with me that often the source we use to recharge utterly and completely fails us? Whether it's more shopping, friends time, Netflix, work, food, meds, holidays, or alone time, it won't fill us up. Have you noticed that those are fun and at times good, but eventually they can't cover that ache and emptiness that we want so badly to fill?

I know that some of you feel that the Source I've been talking about, Jesus, has failed you and that He certainly isn't enough. I have been there myself. I encourage you to get alone and pour out your guts to Him. Ask Him to reveal to you where He was during that season, day, moment of tremendous suffering. This is an exercise Beth Moore had us do in her Bible study, *Believing God²*. I can testify that if you face the pain-filled memories, He will meet you and reveal how His presence was there in that traumatic time. It's messy and terrifying, but also brave and freeing to do this. It takes tremendous courage and patience, but if you cannot believe that Jesus is your reliable Source, then you cannot truly fly free.

Please stop and do this now. Text some friends for prayer support, then let it all out before Him. End this battle with doubt by being honest. Let Him meet you in His time and His way. As you do, you will come to believe that He is for you, not against you, that He has called you and equipped you to fly free amid life's chaos. I'll be praying, and I promise that the pain of facing those memories will be worth coming back to the realization that God is your Source.

CHAPTER 4

Frenemy

"Christ has set us free to live a free life, so take your stand!
Never again let anyone put a harness of slavery on you."

(Galatians 5:1, The Message)

"Stupid battle," I muttered to myself.

On the heels of hearing that my oldest brother's cancer was progressing, I spent time with a little boy whose mom had just died, a lady whose sister had just passed, and a woman who was grieving the passing of her dad. My response to all the pain was to rant about being a part of the stupid battle. I know it's not the nicest thing to say, but that is where I was at - and am at on more days and in more moments than I care to admit. As I analyzed my emotions of sadness and frustration, a few facts dared to show themselves:

We are all in battle: good versus evil.

We are in battle whether we like it or not.

If we are Christians, we are on the winning side whether we feel it or not.

We have a choice: We can fight this raging war, or we can attempt to ignore the battle.

Battle. Never a fun word. It's one thing to have a victory in our walk with God and feel pumped about it. It's another thing to be slugging through an onslaught of arrows pointed at us and our loved ones by the Enemy.

The reality is that when we chose to become Christians, we switched sides. I believe the word used for that in battle terms is "traitor." Satan is furious, and he knows his days are numbered. He is doing everything in his power to immobilize all of us who have chosen to believe God for His gift of salvation. Hence the battle.

I am not a conflict type of girl. I prefer peace to trenches, weapons, and warfare. But like it or not, I am in battle. Satan would love for me to believe whatever lies he pushes my way, to render me "dead weight" in battle. We have a choice to make. We can accept the role of warrior in this epic battle, believe God has won the victory, and use the tools that God has provided us to fight in this war that is raging, or we can attempt to hide from the realities around us.

I have discovered that hiding doesn't work. The bad stuff remains all around me, and if I try to escape, I feel empty and depressed. I am slowly learning that I may as well accept the garbage in this life-time for what it is: battle.

Nothing can keep us from this battle, so it is best to believe our God when He says that: "I, (insert your name), can do all things through Him who strengthens me." (Philippians 4:13).

It is best to believe our God when He says:

"No temptation has overtaken you that is not common to man. God is faithful, and He will not let you be tempted beyond your ability, but with the temptation He will also provide the way that you may be able to endure it." (1 Corinthians 10:13).

"In this world, you will have tribulation, but take heart, I have overcome the world." (John 16:33b).

It is best to believe that God knows what we need to get through each battle, each day and that He will, "equip you with everything good that you may do His will, working in you that which is pleasing in his sight." (Hebrews 13:21).We can rant all we want against the garbage that happens down here, but it only invites defeat and weariness into our lives and does nothing to stop the war from raging.

I have learned that if I look to my Redeemer, Deliverer, Savior, Fortress and Strength, then I will receive what I need to fight well. With my eyes on my Savior, I am free to fight confidently and in a way that leaves me empowered. In the end, God will finish the war, but in the everyday, there are hundreds of battles:

Will we fight anxiety or accept its sucker punch?

Will we choose to be thankful or let the Enemy slip us the poison of a complaining spirit?

Will we stab the spirit of defeat and free the Spirit of peace?

Will we spend time with our Commander and receive the instruction we need or run blindly into the trap that awaits?

If we really want to live the life of victory, we must acknowledge that we are in battle and have an Enemy. Satan is tricky, and the lies he shoots at us may sound friendly. Do any of the following sound familiar?

"Well, you are tired, and they are being insensitive."
"Yeah, let them have it. You have worked so hard for this,
and they are trying to get in your way."
"They really are out to get you, and after all you have
done for them."
Just like in the Garden of Eden, his lies often contain a
hint of truth. God clearly stated that Adam and Eve could
eat from all the fruit in the garden except one. When Satan
tempted Eve, he questioned what God had said, undermining
God's integrity and authority. By taking the truth that they
weren't to eat from one tree, Satan twisted it when he asked,
"Did God really say, 'You must not eat the fruit from any tree
in the garden'?" (Genesis 3:1b).

We must watch out for this trick. Our frenemy is really
the enemy dressing up his lies to entice us to act in ways that
benefit him. As you and I become more aware of our triggers,
it is valuable to realize that there is an angle Satan always wants
us to take. It is the blame angle. When we choose to view our
triggers through this angle we end up blaming our actions on
others. We attempt to free ourselves from personal responsibility, and in doing so, we wrap chains around ourselves.

How can we fly if we believe it's everyone else's fault that
we don't have self-control? How can we stop freaking out
when we think someone else made us do it?

"Stay alert! Watch out for your great enemy, the devil.
He prowls around like a roaring lion, looking for someone
to devour." (1 Peter 5:8, NLT).

Let me assure you that he would absolutely love to devour
you and me, the traitors. We, after all, are on his enemy's team.
Satan knows his time is limited. He knows Jesus has declared
Himself Overcomer. He knows that all Jesus speaks is truth
because Jesus is the Way, the Truth, and the Life (John 14:6).

We had better believe that he is out to get us. He is going
to come sneaking around us with dressed up lies. He wants to
look like our friend so he can lead us into emotional, mental,

and physical bondage. He is the father of lies. Lies are his specialty! What will we do about it? Pretend the battle isn't real? Blame ourselves for the battle?

No!

It's time to get angry, and I mean ANGRY!!!!

If you have never watched the movie *War Room*[3] with Priscilla Shirer, I highly encourage you to do so. I watched it again recently and was inspired by the "anger scene." I know that sounds crazy but let me explain. The anger scene is when Shirer's character comes to understand in a deep way that Satan is out to get her and her family. She gets ANGRY! I call it righteous, God-given anger. I call it her warrior rising up! She starts claiming all that God has given her, and that includes the authority to resist the devil so that he will flee from her as it states in James 4:7. She charges through her house, yelling at the devil to get out and not come back. It is a powerful example of what is ours for the taking.

"For God has not given us the spirit of fear and timidity, but of power, love, and self-discipline." (2 Timothy 1:7, NLT).

Too often I let myself stay chained to fear instead of saying, "No more!!! spirit of fear, be gone in the name of Jesus! Spirit of power, love and self–discipline, come on in!" My dear friends, the time has come. The time is now. It's time for us to reclaim the ground that the enemy has stolen with his friendly lies. It is time to fight him off with the truth of Jesus.

Are there any freedom-killers holding us captive? Are we believing any lies Satan has thrown our way? All through Scripture, God states: He is mighty, He is for us, He gives strength to the weak, He has equipped us to live godly lives, and that He has called us to cast our worries on Him!

Will we choose to remain overwhelmed and tired in spirit because it's easier than searching the Word for the promises of God?

Will we choose to allow freak-outs in our lives because we are tired and overwhelmed, or will we look for God's freedom-builders that enables us to fly free no matter how we are feeling?

It is entirely up to us. And let me tell you something: We can bet Satan is hoping we decide it's not possible, that it's too much work. But we can also bet that Jesus is cheering for us, even interceding on our behalf, praying that we will choose to fight and live out the freedom He died to give us. Check out what the Bible says about how we have been equipped for the battle and how the battle will end.

> Finally, be strong in the Lord and in the strength of his might. Put on the whole armor of God, that you may be able to stand against the schemes of the devil. For we do not wrestle against flesh and blood, but against the rulers, against the authorities, against the cosmic powers over this present darkness, against the spiritual forces of evil in the heavenly places. Therefore take up the whole armor of God, that you may be able to withstand in the evil day, and having done all, to stand firm. Stand therefore, having fastened on the belt of truth, and having put on the breastplate of righteousness, and as shoes for your feet, having put on the readiness given by the gospel of peace. In all circumstances take up the shield of faith, with which you can extinguish all the flaming darts of the evil one; and take the helmet of salvation, and the sword of the Spirit which is the word of God, praying at all times in the Spirit, with all prayer and supplication. To that end keep alert with all perseverance, making supplication for all the saints. (Ephesians 6:10-18).

> And the devil who had deceived them was thrown into the lake of fire where the beast and the false prophet

were, and they will be tormented day and night forever and ever. (Revelation 20:10).

Then I saw a new heaven and a new earth, for the first heaven and the first earth had passed away, and the sea was no more...'Behold, the dwelling place of God is with man. He will dwell with them, and they will be his people, and God himself will be with them as their God. He will wipe away every tear from their eyes, and death shall be no more, neither shall there be mourning, nor crying, nor pain anymore, for the former things have passed away.' (Revelation 21:1, 3b-4).

The sting of death is sin, and the power of sin is the law. But thanks be to God, who gives us the victory through our Lord Jesus Christ. Therefore, my beloved brothers, be steadfast, immovable, always abounding in the work of the Lord, knowing that in the Lord your labor is not in vain. (1 Corinthians 15:56,57).

May the warrior within us rise up and battle anything keeping us from all that God has for us.

CHAPTER 5

Chains No More

*"But the Scriptures declare that we are all prisoners of sin,
so we receive God's promise of freedom only
by believing in Jesus Christ."*

(Galatians 3:22, NLT)

Should, should, should... As the list of "shoulds" came to mind, so did the chains of doubt and condemnation. Guilt surrounded me with crippling force, causing fear and dread to rear their ugly heads. Fear, dread, guilt, doubt, and condemnation were the chains I wrestled with daily. I was exhausted, frustrated, close to despair as I dragged these chains around every day, never able to experience for any length of time with true peace, rest, joy, or life because really, "I should..."

I'm pretty sure you know what I am talking about. I bet that at any given moment, each one of us could rattle off a list of things we feel we should be doing or should be stopping in our lives. Can you believe "should" used to be semi-motivational for me? If I should, and then I fulfill the "should," I must be getting ahead somehow, some way. The problem is that the list never ends. It will have us running every moment from dawn to dusk, and we will still have the nagging feeling that we should have. This, my friends, is bondage, and it will not allow us to fly free. Instead, it will always leave us fettered to chains of doubt, self-condemnation, and many other wing clippers.

I didn't recognize the strength of these chains in my life until a college teacher gently led me to the realization.

Because I'd been a Christian since I was little, and I'm a born-organized type of girl with a deep streak of perfectionism, I had been faithfully doing my daily time with Jesus for years already. I received the Model Student Award in grade 8 and was baptized in grade 9. All this is to say that I was a pretty good follower. I did desire to have a real relationship with Jesus, but mostly I stayed on the straight and narrow road out of fear of disappointing myself, my family, and Jesus.

I must confess that as a youngster, I followed rules out of a guilt so heavy, my heart would quake at the thought of having to feel it. Even when I managed to follow the rules as close to the letter of the law as I could, I would still struggle with gut-wrenching guilt. This time it was because I knew that I had some pride in being such a great rule follower.

A story from my childhood gives a perfect example of the guilt I experienced:

My family would help at a camp that had a strict lights-out rule. If anyone talked after the bell, you would have to come forward in the morning and confess. The staff had no idea how intensely this rule would create torment within me. I would lay in bed wondering if I was breathing in a way that may equate to talking. I would vacillate over whether or not I should confess in the morning. I now know how ridiculous this was, but at the time it was real bondage for me.

After years of struggling with rules and guilt, it was a tremendous gift from God when in college, my Christian

Living professor, Wayne Tomalty, directed me to read a book that would change my life.

I was not only an eager student, I was also one of the college custodians, and while I was in his office collecting garbage one day, he asked if I had selected a book for an assignment in his class. I hadn't, although I had eyed up a thin book I thought would help me get the assignment done quickly. He suggested that I read *The Grace Awakening*[4] by Charles R. Swindoll, and though its length depressed me, I read it. Days passed, and Wayne asked me how the book was going. I blurted out that it was making me angry.

"Good," he responded with what I'm certain was a mischievous twinkle in his eye.

He recognized a Pharisee when he saw one, and he knew I needed to read further to let the truth of God's grace penetrate my legalistic ways. I had been doing the Christian life all wrong by daily purposing in my heart to follow the rules. I attempted to become a better person by using a personal list of failures to motivate myself to try harder.

My way of living the Christian life did not even remotely resemble what the Christian life really is. And it hurt to realize all my attempts at righteous deeds, "are nothing but filthy rags." (Isaiah 64:4, NLT), useless and pride-filled. It was through that book that my eyes began to see Jesus as truly loving me, wanting me to have a daily relationship with Him in which my job was to simply bask in His undeserved love for me. Unconditional love that stays the same even when we blow it; love that doesn't condemn us, but invites us to confess our mess, then be cleansed and free to dance with joy at God's never-ending forgiveness of our sin.

Wayne could see that the shackles of pride encompassing me would only be shattered by the truth that God's grace alone was all that could ever save me. It was so hard to accept this truth, it is a truth I still struggle with at times, but each year I grow in believing it more fully.

He could also see that I had been using my list of "shoulds" as a measurement that I was indeed a good little Christian. I was faced with the fact that I was bound to chains of my own making - chains that kept me from enjoying the abundant life Christ died to give me, chains that kept me freaking out instead of flying free.

I began my jail break in 1999. After having a conversation with someone, I caught myself going over the conversation in my mind, trying to figure out what I ought to have said differently. Now this isn't necessarily a horrible practice, but when it is a habit after every conversation, it is bondage. In doing this over and over, I was constantly doubting that God was at work through me. That did not enable me to enjoy His grace and freedom. I have grown over the years in my ability to spot "shoulds" that attempt to creep back into my life. Now I'm able to view them as the freedom-killers they really are.

"Should" always comes with internal pressure causing our motivation to be skewed. We act on "shoulds" out of guilt, dread and fear. When we are saying "yes" to something God has planned for us, a "should" will not be involved. There will be a desire or nudging in the heart that won't go away until we obey. Our compliance will come out of our relationship with Him not because we believe that if we don't comply we are a horrible person. With obedience comes confidence, joy, and tremendous freedom of spirit because we know we are where we are called to be, doing what He wants us to do.

My list of "shoulds" still tries to be in charge, but God has opened my eyes to the fact that as I immerse my body, soul, and mind in His unending grace, I am free to fly.

"I'm learning to lean, learning to lean, learning to lean on Jesus; finding more power than I'd ever dreamed; I'm learning to lean on Jesus." The words of this song, written by John Stallings[5] years ago, greatly bless me.

I am learning that when I am accepting of His love for me, I can feel myself basking in His grace. Things are flowing in life, and priorities are in place. Bumps in the road are doable because I am "leaning on Him." Eventually, however, the subtle shift begins. I start to think that I can only remain in the dance if I am doing things right or if my heart is changing a little faster. Unfortunately, I begin leaning out of grace and back into the "if I try harder, He'll love me more" trap. My proud heart says, "I think if I do this, I can improve on God's plan and be less dependent on Him."

And the internal dialogue begins:

"His way is too easy."

"I read, 'Accept His grace and live moment-by-moment with Him leading you.' But really? What if I miss His leading?"

"Are you sure that is all He wants from you? What about the verses in the Bible about acting differently? Being quick to listen? You suck at that!"

"What about casting your cares on Him? You never obey Him fully, how can you just receive His grace? It doesn't make sense."

"It's not fair to Him; you should be trying harder."

As these lies begin to penetrate my thinking, my focus slowly shifts from Jesus my Savior to myself, and I fall. I fall into sin. Can you relate?

A pastor once defined sin as doubting God's goodness. Whenever we don't believe that God's perfect way of redemption is enough, sin comes in full force, and with it are all kinds of ugliness. However, God graciously disciplines us, and then it is our choice to repent and turn from our pride or to continue to try to fix Almighty God's perfect plan.

The struggle reminds me of a preschooler in need of obedience boot camp. His reaction to consequences is often to run around the house ranting and breaking things. Sometimes the little one needs to be restrained from doing the "run and rant." A struggle takes place. The young child is eager to get away from me and what I represent. And I attempt to stay calm keeping the fighter contained until he begrudgingly murmurs his apology. Our relationship is restored, and with it order and joy return.

I am just like that youngster when I am in the throes of working for grace, I am in disobedience to God's perfect plan. Discipline ensues, along with the struggle to receive it. To acknowledge my pride is hard; to let go of it is painful. To move from the shame of my forever wandering back into His grace is often where I get stuck. He patiently waits for me as I flail, fuss, and fret, and finally I start to wonder if He loves me. I begin to look back and see what has led me to this state, and as I do, my heart leans back into His grace.

As Ann Voskamp says in her book *One Thousand Gifts*[6], acknowledging grace leads to thanksgiving, which leads to joy, which precedes miracles - the miracle of once again being restored to a deep and intimate relationship with my Abba; the miracle of enjoying stillness and listening for His words of love and encouragement; the miracle of His peace, joy, and power for whatever is to come.

I don't think the cycle will ever be completely broken down here. While I am on earth, I will always struggle with walking in His grace - His way versus my pride, my plans, my way. I am encouraged that I will grow in receiving His grace as He brings me to completion (Philippians 1:6). I will start to flail less and get on my knees in repentance faster.

I am also slowly learning to believe what God told Paul in 2 Corinthians 12:9: "My grace is sufficient (or enough) for you. My power is made perfect in weakness." (parentheses added) Because God's grace is enough, I set my hope fully on that grace that has been brought to me by the revelation of Jesus Christ, according to 1 Peter 1:13.

To think that our awesome, all-knowing Creator would redeem us, knowing all that would ensue, makes my heart soar with thanksgiving, and joy. Remember, Beloved, "You are a chosen race, a royal priesthood, a holy nation, a people for his own possession, that you may proclaim the excellencies of him who called you out of the darkness into his marvelous light." (1 Peter 2:9).

So, friends, it's up to us. Will we acknowledge the chains that are keeping us from flying free and allow ourselves to get drenched in God's grace again? The choice is ours: chains or freedom.

None of us deserves His mind-blowing grace, but let's not allow our stupid pride to keep us chained. Let's run to His open arms and receive the grace He offers no matter how messed up we are, and let's begin to truly live the abundant life He bought for us with His own Son's blood. I want all God has for me. How about you?

God declared in His word, "For he who has been set free will be free indeed." (John 8:36). I'm choosing to daily believe this. Will you, too? When we do, we will be set free to fly in the sureness of His awesome, unending love. What an awesome God we have! He provides a freedom-builder for every single freedom-killer we encounter down here.

CHAPTER 6

Alive Versus Thrive

"We are in love. We are in freedom.
We are in hope, for we are in Jesus."

Anonymous

I lay in bed again. Another day of wanting to get up and go. Another day of my body saying, "No."

As a wife and mother of four, bed was not the ideal location for my list of "to-dos" to be accomplished, yet fatigue was so deep that lifting the sheet off my body was a challenge. On this depressing day where the fatigue made anything but stillness impossible, I cried. I questioned my Source. "Why? Why did you bother letting me be a mom if I can't even be a mom to our babies, but I have to ship them off for someone else to take care of?"

"YOU BRING ME GLORY," came to my mind.

"What? How?" I demanded.

"SIMPLY BY BEING HERE."

"Why?" I fumed with angry tears sliding down my cheeks.

"BECAUSE I MADE YOU."

That was a powerful moment in my journey with God. I fought against that truth. I so desperately wanted to "do" even though He told me that nothing needed to be done. How was that even possible?

I was so very tired of not getting to be the mom I had imagined I would be -full of fun, energy, eagerly playing with our kids, and having other moms over for coffee. I was so sick of not being able to experience so many of my dreams. Instead, I was living life in the frustrating uncertainty of how many hours my body would work in a day. I was left wondering when a fatigue attack would hit, rendering me unable to walk or speak. I seldom felt alive, and when I did it was short-lived as my body would suddenly decide I'd "lived" enough for that day, so off to bed it would send me.

I wanted to thrive, not just be alive. But to me, thriving meant getting items ticked off my list. Thriving was acting on my dream of being an active mom with four kids. For year, I wrestled with my desire to be more actively involved with our children and my inability to do so. I was so full of despair and sorrow. I just wanted to get out of this awful, hard place of helplessness.

I began to have suicidal thoughts. These brief but terrifying moments of wanting to end my life rocked me to the core. I would talk myself out of acting on the thought, but guilt ensued for having thought it in the first place. I created boundaries to help myself not act on these thoughts and eventually I began to share with my trusted ones where I was really at.

I chose to go for counselling, see my doctor, and go on an antidepressant. As the truth came out and these helpful tools began to take effect, my body, mind, and soul began to heal. I remember vividly a powerful moment in which I was on the floor in our bedroom. I was crying out in prayer, wrestling with heart-wrenching self-condemnation, when God asked me to look up. I was terrified. I had been face-down on the ground. I was afraid to look up, because I was so ashamed that I had somehow gotten so depressed. I felt deserving only of condemnation, but when I obeyed, He poured out His grace on me.

"I LOVE YOU. YOU ARE MINE," He whispered confidently to my heart.

My heart wanted to believe, but I struggled to accept those life-changing words.

I believe this is a normal situation for each of us. When we are offered unconditional love, we tend to be guilt-ridden or skeptical or both. We wrestle with this concept because it is not often a part of our human existence.

The following portion is a blog post[7] from when my husband sustained a concussion, which led to a neurosurgeon doing special testing on his brain. As you read this personal account, see if it resonates with your experiences of profound grace:

Today we woke up at the crack of dawn and went to the hospital. Calvin got suited up. I told him to have a good nap. Then I left him and sat in the sun to wait.

I think I had my emotions in lock-down because I knew I had hours of waiting ahead of me. The lyrics, "While I'm waiting, I will praise you,"[8] ran through my brain. Somewhere in that song it talks about being bold and confident. I wasn't feeling those things, but there was some peace amid the waves. I recognized that peace to be Jesus. He was and is my peace. I felt His presence there as I listened to Chris Tomlin's song, *With Me*[9]. The song is all about how when we know we are with God, we can go through anything, and I found it to be true in that moment.

After a little more than an hour, the phone rang. It was the recovery room. Calvin was awake, and the surgeon wanted to talk to us. Thankfully I had little time to ponder the *why* of the call that came "too soon." I got back to the recovery room as quickly as possible. The surgeon explained that they were able to get a clearer look at the unique area of Calvin's brain before they did any procedure. What they had thought was a problem was really no problem at all, so they woke him up and took him to recovery.

We are now back at our room, and I'm trying to digest the doctor's words.

"What?! Wow!! What?!" my ever-analyzing mind declares. "How did they not figure this out sooner? Are they absolutely certain we are ok? Wow! There really will be no major recovery time. Wow, the 'brain journey' is done, is it?" Questions and ponderings roll through my head.

I feel pressure to be thrilled, but there is a piece of me that is leery. Call it fear, cynicism or being tired, but there are still some "what-ifs" in my mind. I think it is probably normal to feel this way - it's how I usually feel about a huge outpouring of God's grace.

There's a myriad of emotions rolling within. I feel small and undeserving. I feel sad for those who feel they haven't experienced His grace today, not in a huge way or even in a small way. I am worried for those who have been asked to persevere without a miracle even though they have been asking longer and for harder things. I feel silly for not cheering loudly. I think I am in shock.

He said, "Yes," to little old me. He heard me as I wept in my closet alone, full of terror at the possible outcomes. He said, "Yes," to the prayers of my beautiful friends who surrounded me moments before kids' club started on the first night we had become aware of the doctor's concerns with Calvin's brain. He said, "Yes," to me when I was too weak to go through all this last month. He didn't have to, but He chose to say, 'Yes,' to healing my amazing husband's brain.

Just this week, a friend prayed, asking God to show us a lavish display of His grace during our time here in Edmonton. Yes!

Months ago, an aunt declared that she would pray that the surgeon would look at Calvin's brain and determine all was well. Yes!

My mom prayed that we would be spared from the enemy's attacks on this day. Yes!

Today I felt like I couldn't pray "for real," that all my prayers had already been said, and now it was a matter of waiting and seeing what God would do. And today He decided, "Yes!" was the best for us in this situation.

I am still in shock! We had been trying for plans A and B, but there was a plan C. And it was better, not worse than our plans! But that is how God works, isn't it? He goes and does what we couldn't or wouldn't let ourselves dream about. He pours His grace on our hearts that struggle to believe, hope, and wait. Why? Because He is God and He is good! Our God is generous in His gifts to us! Second Corinthians talks about how God is the God of all comfort (1:3). "All" - I love that! My God is in charge of *all* comfort. That means He will give it to all who ask. Verse 5 says, "For as we share abundantly in Christ's sufferings, so through Christ we share abundantly in comfort too." Our God is not stingy; He will provide. Verse 20 tells us that "all the promises of God find their Yes in Him." What He says, He will do. We can trust Him!

This was an extravagant display of God's grace toward us in such a hard year. It was painful to go through the waiting, the wondering. It was also a challenge to see if we would trust Him no matter what the outcome was. It was through that trying time that God has stretched us, grown us, challenged us to choose to believe who He is. And when He responded with a miracle, I could hardly believe it. Faith is believing even when you don't see the answer on the way.

My purpose in sharing this story is to convey how weird grace can feel, yet how amazing it is all at the same time. It is often hard to believe that God can truly remove all our sin

- past, present, and future, and that He loves the real us that is covered in filth. It is weird, yet amazing, all at the same time.

I was in the midst of my on-going health struggles, in which my faith was already being tested, when this story took place. I don't know why God allowed it to happen, but I do know this: He used it to help me more deeply pursue a life in which I would thrive because I chose to believe Him.

If you ever have this tricky feeling: uncertainty whether you are believing God or not, ask Him to use it to draw you closer to Him. He will--in a way unique to you. It is impossible to truly thrive and fly free if we do not fully believe our Source. Thankfully, God graciously provides what we need and knows exactly when we are ready to receive it. For me it was through a Bible study our church offered: *Believing God* by Beth Moore[10]. God used its message to fan a flame in my heart that wanted to fly free.

There was no way for me to live with a chronic illness and fly free unless I believed my God when He said He would provide all that I need. (Philippians 3:19) My prayer was often, "Lord, help me believe." I took great encouragement from the father in the gospel of Mark, who prayed, "I do believe, but help me overcome my unbelief!" (Mark 9:24, NLT). Jesus' response to him was so tender!

Over the years, my God-given desire to thrive has grown louder and louder. With this desire has also come the resolve to choose to believe God no matter what life throws at me - even if my plan for the day is messed up, even if I am exhausted or my body decides to sideline me.

During my years of fatigue, I suffered many losses. And yet, as I look back, I can see the faithful hand of Almighty God growing me, teaching me, preparing me, and grooming me to become the victorious warrior He has always seen me to be. And you know what? That's how He views you too!

Will you acknowledge the areas in your life where you are simply alive but not actually thriving?

Will you ask Him what you have stopped believing about Him and allow Him to heal that wounded place in your heart?

I've discovered as I grow stronger in believing God that I am more able to fly free consistently. I've learned that I can lay down my attempts to "do" and simply be loved and accepted by Him in a way that sets my heart free to fly, no matter what my circumstances.

I count it a privilege that He would instruct me to write this book on freedom, not because I always fly free - I don't - but because this is part of what He's taught me in my many years of waiting for healing. God has shown me that we really can fly free no matter what our bodies, minds, or souls say.

It's in connecting daily with my Source that I am reminded that I am only ever fully alive and able to thrive when my identity is based on Him - who He is, and who He says I am. The minute I choose not to believe what He says is the minute I begin my descent from flying free to freaking out. So, it is a daily choice, an hourly choice even. Will I freak out over this or that or will I choose to believe what my Source says about Himself, this situation, and me?

Oh friend, it would take a whole book and beyond to share the truth of His love and character with you, the power and purpose Almighty God has for you. As much as I'd like to, I can't do your ground work for you. I can't force you to choose to believe God is your Source. I can't make you do self-checks that help you discern your triggers or what you may not be believing about God.

Because of my own experience, I can, however, promise that the work is worth the fruit it bears. There is no doubt in my mind that as you allow yourself to say yes to God, spend time in honest communication with Him, and read about Him in His Word, the Bible, you will be forever changed. Your passion to thrive will grow.

I encourage you to ask Him to open your heart and mind, to give you the ability to believe Him and His Word. Immerse yourself in His promises and the truth of how He views you. If we've received Jesus' gift, His death on the cross for us, we are new creations in Christ, fully forgiven.

At a Beth Moore event, she had us stand and declare our identity in Christ. This is such a valuable exercise. Here is the declaration:

I am a woman of God, redeemed by Jesus Christ,
Loved, pursued, and chosen, empowered with words of life,
Clothed in strength and dignity, commissioned here and now,
Gifted by the Spirit, forgiven and unbound.
Blessed is she who believes!!!

I highly recommend you write this out and post it where you will see it often. Let the words soak in so you remember each one. Then, when the enemy of your soul comes to stifle your ability to thrive (and believe me he will try, and often!), you will be prepared with these truths.

When faced with the enemy or our own internal resistance, we can pray our identity. It may sound something like this:

"Ok, so it says I am pursued by You, but I don't feel pursued. I feel forsaken. Please help me to believe You. Help me see how You have pursued me and are pursuing me. Thank You, Amen."

Because He has connected with me, I know He will connect with you, too. He repeatedly promises in His Word that He will draw near to those who draw close to Him. (James 4:8) He will reveal Himself to those who will seek Him. We can believe that our living, active, power-filled Source doesn't want us to just hang in there barely feeling alive. No, He wants us to experience real life in Him - the Source of all life.

As we invest our time choosing to grow and opening ourselves up to Him, we will be able to thrive, to fly free, even when the enemy whispers a lie into our ears, when a goal is blocked, or a dream shut down for a season. This is because we won't be dependent on what we have done. Instead, we will be focused on who God is and all that He has done for us. This will cause our spirits to truly thrive.

CHAPTER 7

Do I have To?!?!

"Anything that makes me need God is a blessing."
-Nancy Leigh DeMoss

The emotions had been building and building, and then one fateful day the dam broke. It was a big reaction for a non-confrontational kid. It was a huge reaction for a sixth-grade girl who was trying so hard to do life perfectly.

It had been six years of one mini incident after another that compounded into that reaction. I don't even recall what the girl said to me on that day, but I was certain condescension and disdain resided in her words. With this conviction, all the anger, resentment, and bitter jealousy that I had been containing for years burst out.

SLAP!

My hand stung. My heart dropped. My eyes grew huge. I had done it. I had actually slapped the most popular girl in school across the face - and hard!

SLAP!

A nanosecond passed, and my slap was returned, sending me running away from Miss Popular with my cheek stinging, mind racing, and nose bleeding.

Unforgiveness. If left to fester, it will result in an eruption or suffocation that will deeply affect its holder. Unforgiveness is a freedom-stealer as old as time. Its antidote is, of course, forgiveness. The very word forgiveness can cause a victim's blood to chill or boil.

Forgiveness: The laying down of my right to accuse, "to pardon or acquit of sins."[11] The tricky part about forgiveness is that we can be so eager to be forgiven, but we aren't always eager to forgive.

When Miss Popular and I sat in the principal's office facing judgement for our actions, I didn't necessarily care about being forgiven. I cared about not getting the strap. Yes, this was back in the olden days. I was scared about telling my parents and about what the consequences would be.

I was willing to forgive Miss Popular because she had simply reacted to my rage. She likely had no idea how I had been harboring a grudge against her for six years. My desire for her to really forgive me was not in the principal's office. We "forgave" each other that day because it was the path of least resistance. However, one day in grade seven, I experienced an urgency to be truly forgiven by her.

It was our first Language Arts class in the junior high building, a thrilling new beginning in a new place. Our lovely Language Arts teacher introduced the opportunity for journaling. As we spent time in class journaling, we were able to write about anything. We could even write to her if we wanted. I was thrilled with this idea, then horrified as I realized that Miss Popular was in my class and could easily share with our new teacher that hideous incident back in elementary school. My reputation would be ruined even before this new season of my life began. My desire to be liked by my new L.A. teacher outweighed my pride, so with my heart in my throat, I approached Miss Popular and requested that neither of us write about the slap incident. She agreed, and I was so relieved.

Being truly forgiven is such a relief! The weight of the wrong I inflicted on another is lifted. The relationship is set right and I can fly again, provided I don't fall for the condemnation or guilt trap.

To forgive is another story - a harder one, I find. In order to forgive, I have to be willing to lay down my lists of the wrongs done against me. This can be very difficult.

For those of you who were abused in any way, I can only imagine how absolutely miraculous it is to have been able to forgive your offender. Or maybe you haven't. Maybe you are wrestling with knowing that you need to, but you are unsure how. Hugs to you my friend. I pray that you will continue to bring this before God, asking Him, the One who has been wronged the most, to enable you to do this tremendously hard thing.

In her book *Fervent*, Priscilla Shirer talks about unforgiveness as a strategy the Devil uses. "He wants you baking in unforgiveness until spiritual life is hard and crisp around the edges. Lifeless. Comatose. But Jesus...He wants you free. That's what He created you for."[12]

I know there is freedom in forgiveness. My life bears witness of this. Forward growth has always entailed acknowledging areas of unforgiveness in my heart, then choosing to be obedient to God's command that we forgive others as He has forgiven us. Matthew 6 clearly states this is a requirement in our relationship with Jesus. How can we reflect Him if we are unwilling to forgive those who wrong us?

Take heart, dear friend. Every freedom-producer given by God will be lived out by His Spirit at work in us. We can walk in forgiveness because Christ will enable us to forgive. If you are struggling with forgiveness, will you ask Him today to help you become willing?

Will you ask Him to grow in you a desire to forgive or be forgiven so that you can truly be in deep relationship with Him and others?

Will you ask Him to remove the stigma of what you think forgiveness is and replace it with what He says it is?

Will you ask Him to reveal to you the worth of forgiveness and why it is essential to flying free?

Recently I became aware that I was keeping a mental list of someone's "sins against me." The poor soul didn't have a clue that he was on trial every single day. Eventually as my focus continued to be fixated on his wrong-doings, the Holy Spirit opened my heart to see how I was sabotaging my relationship with this dear one as well as with my God. When I spent time with God going through the perceived wrongs, forgiving myself and the other member, then receiving His gift of forgiveness toward me, my heart was again able to dance.

Romans 5:8 states that while we were at our "ugliest," most sinful, Christ died for us. He didn't wait for us to clean up first. He was completely aware of all our sins - past, present, and future - and He still chose to die in our place so that we can be forgiven and made right in His Father's eyes.

There is no better place to be than forgiven by God Almighty. This allows us untold privileges and blessings which include access to all the freedom-builders He offers. If we have accepted His forgiveness, then we have full access to the Creator of the Universe. We are able and encouraged to "come boldly to the throne of our gracious God. There we will receive his mercy, and we will find grace to help us when we need it most." (Hebrews 4:16, NLT).

If this isn't freedom, then what is?

Are you having difficulty with forgiveness? Has this chapter seemed like a bitter pill to swallow? I pray that you will allow God into your inner struggle. I pray that you will take the step of obedience towards forgiveness so that you can enjoy your freedom. The one who has wronged you so deeply will have to face God one day. Why not place their wrong-doing in the hands of God so you can enjoy the freedom and healing He has for you right here, right now? It may not be an instant thing. It may not feel like freedom or even real forgiveness at first. But I believe that as you talk this through with God, asking Him for help to forgive, He will answer. Step by step, He will enable you to truly soar freely.

As Priscilla Shirer shares in her book *Fervent*, "Genuine freedom and renewed fervency are waiting for you on the other side of forgiveness. And the forgiveness you don't have any desire to give right now can be amazingly enabled through prayer. When galvanized with the living truth of God's Word, fervent prayer is the bucket that can dip down into the reserves of God's strength and pull up all the resolve you need for releasing other people from what they owe you."[13]

CHAPTER 8

The Pity of Praise

"The truth doesn't defeat me. It sets me free."
~fearfully made mom~

Praise has a way of surprising me. I've read that it has power, but for me it seems to take forcing myself to praise amid heart-wrenching sorrow to feel the depths of that power.

Pity has power too, a lot of power. As Sarah Young shares in her book *Jesus Calling*[14], pity is a slippery slope leading nowhere good. I know this is true. I have dabbled in pity more times than I want to recount, and it has never given me anything but grief. Layers and layers of anger, blame, and dread did nothing to help me face the actual struggle at hand. Instead, pity sucked out the very energy that could have served me well had it been used to read Psalms of praise and thanksgiving amid the ugh.

We are told SO many times in the Bible to give thanks because this is the will of God. Personally, I've often found those verses annoying, especially in the-midst of "learn-to-praise" boot camp.

I don't even know all the sources I should credit for what I've learned, but Sarah Young, Cheree Quantz, and the Bible are most definitely on the list. It is because of these influences that I considered the "why" behind God's invitation/command for us to praise Him amid all circumstances.

We are asked to praise God and be thankful because doing so opens up our hearts to Him. And when our hearts are open, our raw emotions come out, enabling us to become honest, even ugly, with God. When we choose to praise Him despite our feelings, He enables us to release our emotional reactions to life's chaos to Him. By doing this, we are set free to fly because our focus has turned from ourselves back to Him.

We see examples of this throughout the Psalms, a book in the Bible that I, and so many others, love for a very good reason. The writers speak our language. It is here that many, myself included, have learned honesty with God, praise, and thanksgiving. It is here that I have personally learned to lay my heart bare and then make the choice - even though things are brutal - that I will trust my Rock! The pity of praise is that often we choose not to praise because it grates on our desire to sulk.

The pity of praise is that honesty with God is SO powerful to restoring our hope and joy in Christ, yet we often do not believe it will do anything except make us really mad. Maybe we need to get really mad to pour out our hearts to God. He already knows what we are feeling, so we may as well say it and let Him meet us there. When we do, He will shock us again and again with His forgiveness and grace.

I love Psalm 73 where the author shares how frustrated he is that those who don't love God seem to have an easy life. As the Psalm continues, the author begins to hear himself, and he ends like this: "When my soul was embittered, when I was pricked in heart, I was brutish and ignorant; I was like a beast toward you. Nevertheless, I am continually with you; you hold my right hand. You guide me with your counsel, and afterwards you will receive me to glory.... My flesh and my heart may fail, but God is the strength of my heart and my portion forever." (Psalm 73:21-24,26).

Here is a real-life example of the power of praise - a blog post written from my heart in 2015[15]:

So much has changed in our world in so little time. It's wild how a person can wait and wait and wonder when the change will come, and then WHAM it hits and nothing is the same again.

That WHAM came a few weeks back when my brother Byron's tumors suddenly stole his mobility. Nearly overnight, he went from walking and driving to living in a hospital bed and being dependent on others for so much.

One would think that this life altering blow would be insurmountable, but I can testify from my time with Byron last weekend that this WHAM has set him on a war path. He is determined to face this season as an adventure. To finish well. To "ride the snot out of this body." To enjoy his beloveds. To leave nothing unsaid and to encourage and inspire those around him to "live with abandon[16]," all the while holding on to his God for comfort, peace, and strength to endure his tent that is falling apart. How can I give up in the face of such perseverance? How can I complain in the face of such determined living?

The truth is I can't. I've tried to stay grumpy about Byron being moved into hospice yesterday. I mean, what person in their right mind celebrates moving into hospice? But I can't, for the sole reason that Byron is not complaining; he is celebrating, accepting this place where he is at as from God and being thankful that he got into the hospice he wanted and faster than he thought possible.

62

B's always been that way, our family sanguine in the midst of melancholies. God knows we have needed his wild ideas and insane enthusiasm to learn how to enjoy life more fully.

I have been marveling at how God uses the one in the most suffering to challenge and grow those who are watching the suffering. I remember my dear friend's child had died, and we were at their son's funeral. The worship team was singing, *Blessed Be the Name of the Lord*[17]. I remember having just thought something along the line of, "There is no way I am singing that right now; I'm mad at God," when I caught a glimpse of the recently bereaved momma on her knees in worship before her God, and I was smitten with conviction. If the one suffering so deeply chooses to worship, who am I, that from the sideline I would turn my nose up at their offering? I learned an important lesson in that moment that to choose to worship amid my anger and uncertainty is to help my proud, hard heart to come back into fellowship with God.

As I watched, listened and shared with Byron last weekend, I was in awe of God's strength shining through his weakness - how God was speaking through him in the way he treated his staff, precious wife and family, how he spoke into my kids' hearts and wasn't afraid to let tears flow as they rose to the surface, how he savored the good moments and prayed through the hard.

How can I not choose to see the good in this brutal WHAM when it is all around: in the way our family is supporting each other; in the way bondage about emotions and their expression is being broken; in the way my own children are learning about compassion, grief, living well, and choosing to live life as an adventure; how their uncle and his family are choosing to be thankful no matter what WHAM comes and choosing to trust God no matter what.

How can I not rejoice amid the pain? He is at work because we sure couldn't do this without him.

This adventure is so much bigger than what we see.

Our God is mighty and is at work doing mighty things. In less than a year, my uncle has been taken home suddenly, my grandpa has passed into glory, and my brother's cancer has grown with a vengeance. One would think that our family would have the "right" to be angry, bitter, lost, and broken, but if you look and listen, you will hear words of truth and hope and life as our God restores, comforts, and enables us to endure.

Praise to our God who is the only One able to bring lasting beauty out of pain.

Praise to our Lord who is the only One able to cause warriors of truth to rise up out of suffering.

Praise to our God who is the only One able to empower us with a perseverance and faith that we will do this valley well and not give in to the temptations of the devil.

I don't know where you are at or what "adventure" you are facing. Maybe you are at that place I've been more times than I can count in the last month: that messy place where your breaking heart screams, "I don't want to be a part of this. I can't survive this. Please don't make me go through this!" If so, pour it out to Him.

He has a wild way of helping us believe that somehow, some way, He will redeem what has been lost and bring beauty from our pain.

So when the grief hits hard and I want to quit, I'll picture my Byron with tears in his eyes, saying, "Let the tears out, Andy; it's good for you." Or maybe it will be, "It's not what we want, but God has given me such peace." Or perhaps, "I'm gonna ride the snot out of this body," or, "I love you. He's got this adventure."

Personally, I'm at the place that when I hear the word "adventure," I cringe, but I know that the only adventure to be on is God's, so I have a choice: I can snuggle in and let Him rise up through my weakness to do His thing for His glory, or I can be angry and complain, staying trapped in my pain.

Thanks, Big Brother, for leading the way so well and for removing the choice for me. As I see your example of persevering with joy, I know that is the only way I can choose to do this adventure.

> Psalm 46:1-6
> God is our refuge and strength, a very present help in trouble.
> Therefore we will not fear though the earth gives way,
> though the mountains be moved into the heart of the sea,
> though its waters roar and foam,
> though the mountains tremble at its swelling.
> There is a river whose streams make glad the city of God,
> the holy habitation of the Most High.
> God is in the midst of her; she shall not be moved;

God will help her when morning dawns.
The nations rage, the kingdoms totter;
He utters his voice, the earth melts.
The LORD of hosts is with us;
the God of Jacob is our fortress.
Come, behold the works of the LORD,
how he has brought desolations on the earth.
He makes wars cease to the end of the earth;
he breaks the bow and shatters the spear;
he burns the chariots with fire.
"Be still, and know that I am God.
I will be exalted among the nations,
I will be exalted in the earth!"
The LORD of hosts is with us;
the God of Jacob is our fortress.

I wrote the above article in May 2015. My dear, oldest brother, Byron Jonathan Porritt, passed away on September 4, 2015.

During those last months, the worship times Byron and I shared were beyond this world. While in palliative care, Byron was able to be in a wheelchair. On one occasion, Byron, his lovely wife Caroline, and I commandeered a tiny lounge. Caroline had fallen asleep, and By was talking. I was drinking in every word. I remember him sharing his concern as to how Caroline would pay for their kids to continue in the school they attended, and then somehow, we were praying. It wasn't any old praying; it was so strong and so sweet, and God's presence was so thick, I am sure it was God's gift to me: a glimpse of what Heaven will be like when By and I will both be there worshipping our God fully, with our all.

Byron moved from palliative care to hospice. While he was waiting out his final days on earth, knowing we both loved worship, and wanting to enjoy that thick presence of Jesus again with my brother, I turned on my playlist. With tears streaming down our faces as different lyrics struck a chord in our broken hearts, we praised our good God even though He was not giving us the miracle we so desperately wanted. It was a sacred and powerful time. And if it was powerful to me, what must it be like for the enemy who strives to destroy me at every turn? Oh, how we fought off defeat with thanksgiving.

God graciously prepared me for my journey of releasing Byron. He did this by having me read Ann Voskamp's story of her heartbreaking wrestle that led to victory through gratitude in her book *One Thousand Gifts*[18].

As Byron told me again and again throughout his entire life but especially in those last months, "God is good, Andy, all the time. He is so faithful. I just have so much to be thankful for."

Freaking out has its roots in ungratefulness. Somewhere along the line, we feel we didn't get what we deserved, therefore we are entitled to freak out. But where does that reaction really lead us? It leads us to the slippery slope of pity. It is only through God's weapons of praise and thanksgiving that we will not lose our footing and fall into the abyss. Either way, it's work.

It is work to choose thanksgiving amid the pain or to praise after we've wallowed our way into the abyss of pity. So why not use God's freedom-builder to keep pity at bay? Yes, it will be hard and messy, but trust me, my friend, as we choose to praise, though tears may be streaming down our faces, our hearts will begin to feel comfort and His peaceful presence. And it is here our hearts can be freed from the pain they carry.

My last night alone with Byron was a hard one. He was struggling with his increasing lack of mobility. At this point he was only able to use one hand. While I loved on him, he shared his frustration with me. Then he mentioned the song *One Day at a Time* by Cristy Lane[19], so I found it on Youtube. Together we sang it, again and again. "One day at a time, Sweet Jesus....Lord for my sake, teach me to take one day at a time."

Praise has a way of redirecting my focus so that I'm back in His deep presence, filled to the brim with peace and grace.

Later, while By was dozing, I got out my journal and added more things I was thankful for to a list I had previously begun. He woke up and caught me and asked what I was doing. After I told him, he gently grinned and said, "I'd like to see that sometime." I never did get to read it to him. I'm not even sure I got to thank him for his influence of thanksgiving in my life, but he left a tremendous one.

Please, dear ones, will you take time to invest in this powerful freedom restorer? You will not regret your choice. You can simply start by saying five things you are thankful for each morning and again at bedtime. Believe me, investing in this freedom-builder is tremendous protection from so many harmful killers. I pity those who choose not to accept this gift because it truly wields profound power.

Thank you, Abba, for all You do,
Your faithful guidance
and surprises too.
Your grace continues to blow my mind.
Peace in Your presence, I always find.
When I stop and wait, I feel You near
And hear You breathe truth into my ear.
What a gift You are to me
Because of You, I am free to be.
Thank You, Abba, for this day,
Help me to glorify You in what I think, do, and say.
by Andrea Fehr

CHAPTER 9

In Stillness, I Will...

"The highest form of prayer is to stand silently in awe of God."
~St. Isaac the Syrian~

"In stillness, you will..." prompted the TV show host.
"Lose my ever-loving mind?!?!?" queried the responder.

Beep!

"Sorry, wrong answer," the host replied.

This is a make-believe scenario, but what came to mind as you read it? Stillness is something most of us are not good at! It's more common to hear phrases like, "I am overwhelmed!" or, "I am behind and in a panic!"

We all have times when life is completely overwhelming. We are busy, yet others keep vying for our attention. Internal pressures and circumstances can easily create chaos that pushes us toward freaking out. Perhaps you have recently found yourself thinking, "If one more thing happens..." This is usually a strong indicator that panic is gaining control and a freak out is on the way.

Stillness can seem impossible or like a cop-out when we are in pressure- filled situations. The truth is that Satan would love for us to hold these views. He would love for you to disregard this chapter, but God created stillness as a necessary freedom-builder.

Does constant busyness cause you to fly free?

Why not stick around and let me share what God has been teaching me about stillness?

In Part 1, we investigated what our triggers are. It's important to realize that triggers can be masquerading under another name, like "productivity" or "planning." In our house, these two can be code for, "Andrea is frantically trying to gain control in a season of chaos," or what we dub "mission mode." "Sorry, Baby, can't talk right now; Mommy is in mission mode." Am I trying to save the day, or simply myself, from feeling inadequate? Usually it's a bit of both.

I am learning that in order for me to experience peace and joy more frequently, I must pace myself. I am also realizing that when I get into "mission mode," it isn't because God is calling me to get all the things on that list done. It is usually my pride, my desire to please, or fear.

Being motivated to get things done is not wrong, but if our accomplishments become security and source of stress or joy, then we are in trouble. God needs to be our All-in-All, not a completed list or a clean basement.

Pacing ourselves in this journey of life is difficult, especially when people all around us are going a million miles an hour, but it's a freedom-producer worth investing in. It adds longevity to our ability to press on in life. So what helps us set the pace?

Back in college, Calvin and I would occasionally run together. Let's just say that his pace and my pace are not the same. Graciously, he would slow down so that I could survive the workout. It works much the same way in families. Often we compensate for one another by making sure the person who needs more receives it. It is important, however, for each of us to know our personal pace. On the days I feel like I really have my rhythm, why is that? It is also important to accept our pace, even though it is different from those around us.

What does this have to do with stillness? Well, I've discovered that stillness has a way of helping me slow down when I begin to go too fast for my own good or the good of those around me. When I am not pacing myself, things can get out of control fast. When I allow God, the One who designed me, to take charge of my pace, I can relax, knowing He knows what must take place in my day. This sounds like a simple solution, but I'm sure you will find it is easier said than done. The good news is that it is worth it.

God sometimes uses a plethora of circumstances to help us set our pace. It is usually aggravating when circumstances keep us from goals we have for ourselves. Slowly, however, as we accept these "pacing devices," they can help us live a rhythm that is better for us. What a blessing it would be if we truly accepted our limitations as gifts from God that help maintain the pace He intended for us.

Isn't it comforting to know that God always has a way for us to get through whatever struggles we have? He knows that we are dust, and He knows how we function. He is acquainted with our personalities, and He loves our individuality. We can trust Him fully when He tells us to bring our concerns to Him. He has walked this earth and is familiar with the stress of it. He is, after all," founder and perfecter of our faith" (Hebrews 12:2). So, why don't we let Him set our pace? He promises to provide for us, every step of the way.

Pacing, dependence, and stillness may all seem like bad words in the moment. Viewing stillness as the way to reset our pace might seem like an impossibility. If this is what you think, you are not the only one to feel this way. But stay with me and you will begin to see the freedom these words can bring. Before we learn how to add stillness into our lives, let's take a moment and discover what it means personally.

What does the phrase "In stillness, you will..." bring to your mind?

What does "still" even mean these days? Is "still" laying on the couch with your phone? Or without your phone?

Does it classify as "still" if you are laying down, but your mind is racing a mile a minute? What would you like "stillness" to look for you?

When is the last time you felt still in body, mind, and soul? Did you like it? What caused it? Did it feel creepy?

What is your biggest fear when you consider adding stillness into your life?

What is your biggest roadblock in actually implementing stillness into your life?

Stillness from movement has been forced upon me numerous times when I've experienced fatigue attacks so severe, they've rendered me unable to move. Even after resting for long periods of time, watching television, talking on the phone, or simply listening to someone would exhaust me. With the amount of forced fatigue breaks I've had to take, I would have lost it long ago had I not learned how to develop a stillness or slowing down of the mind to some extent.

A psychiatrist once taught me a technique to help slow down my mind and body:

Take a deep breath for as long as possible.
Hold it for as long as possible.
Release it for as long as possible.
Repeat.

This slowing down tool led me to discover that I can't think, worry, or analyze when I am focusing on my breathing. My mind has a slow-down button after all. What wonderful news!

Eventually I added a phrase of Scripture to my breathing exercise.

"I can do all things," HOLD, "through Christ who strengthens me." (Philippians 4:13) Repeat.

Or

"Be still, and know," HOLD, "that I am [he is] God." (Psalm 46 :10 change mine) Repeat.

This was the beginning of me becoming okay with forced stillness, the beginning of finding the gifts in stillness.

Being still is an opportunity to refocus on God. In Psalm 46:10, He invites us to "Be still, and know that I am God." There is a reason He asks us to be still. He knows that in our busyness, we tend to forget He is God. When we are busy, we lose perspective. Stillness is an invitation to reconnect with our Creator--the One who's provided the lungs we use to breathe through each day.

The thought of stillness can seem scary. Even a brief pause from busyness can cause our minds to take us on a rollercoaster ride of panic and stress. Who wants to lay down for that? We buy into the lie that if we stay busy, we will get more things done. If we get more things done, we will be less stressed. But there are always more things to do, and a question worth asking is, "Who or what might we really be hiding from in our busyness?" Are we finding our worth, our security by keeping busy? It's time to face these issues and apply God's freedom plan to them so that we can embrace life instead of race through it.

Once we accept our need for stillness, we have a tremendous opportunity to embrace and enjoy the gift of God's ever-present presence. Learning to become still and enjoy God's presence and peace has been one of the most excellent gifts I've received through my years of illness. Knowing that at any time I can choose to pause my life, if only for a few moments, to talk with and listen to my Creator, has been life-changing for me.

When I first began this listening journey, it felt scary and weird. I remember the first time I sensed God was speaking to my heart. In my uncertainty and need for clarification, I reached out to the professor who had recommended *The Grace Awakening*[20] to me. He said that I was not losing my mind and to receive the gift for what it was, realizing many do not sense God in this way.

If you are one who has not "heard" God in this same way, that's ok. We are all created uniquely, and I don't know what He has in mind for you. I do know, however, as I've set time aside to just be with Him, He has brought me closer to Himself. And He invites you, too, to be obedient in His call to come.

When we do, we not only experience the gift of His presence, we learn to be willing to slow down to offer our presence to others as well. We receive so that we can give. An example of this can be found in the following true story that I posted on my blog[21] of how someone blessed me by sitting with me:

I hadn't planned on this to happen, but then again, I never do... My body "simply" decides that there are enough members who are fatigued within it and then, voila, the attack begins. Sometimes it starts with weak legs, sometimes with a feeling like something is squeezing my throat. No matter how it starts, it basically ends the same way each time: with me utterly exhausted, nearly unable to move or speak. After resting, I regain my strength and eventually return to my "normal," but not without some sadness from the experience or frustration and anxiety about what has gone on.

I found myself in post-attack exhaustion after our church service yesterday. When the service ended, Calvin gave me a questioning look, and I responded with, "Home, I just want to go home," not unlike Diana Barry in *Anne of Green Gables*[22]. We headed toward the exit at the front of the sanctuary, the shortest route to our van. I was pleasantly surprised to discover I could still walk, and by walking, I mean creeping, but still this was a huge improvement from many other attacks. As we reached the door, a dear friend came up beside us and asked if she could help.

It's at times like this that you want to reassure your friend or family member that you are ok, and it looks worse than it feels, but well, it is impossible for my body to talk or even offer a smile of assurance at this stage in the game. Thankfully my husband was there to explain a little about how an attack works. She stayed with us, opening the door as we got to the landing. I sank down in relief while Calvin got the van, and my dear friend sank down beside me.

My eyes still well up with tears at this sacred sitting.

The gift of presence.

A sweet soul joining me in my valley with no way of fixing me, but there just to offer her presence.

Just sitting on that step, feeling her beside me, knowing she cared, hearing her pray while she held my hand, was so comforting. So sacred. It was as connected as anyone could be with me on earth--a sharing of my burden, a decision made to be with me in my darkness without trying to fix me. What a tremendous gift. Thank you, dear one!

To enjoy the gifts stillness can offer, we must choose to be still. I remember struggling with God about the "Be still, and know that I am God."(Psalm 46:10) verse. "Daddy, I don't even know how to 'be,' let alone 'be still.' How am I supposed be able to know that you are God?" I would lament in my all-or-nothing perfectionistic mind-set.

"Just be," He would reply.

"Just come."

"Just show up."

What a beautiful invitation.

Don't let Satan rob you of the freedom-builder that stillness is. Don't let him convince you it is not a Christian practice or that you could never do it. Instead, trust our Creator, your Source, and just attempt to be still with Him.

God is near, wanting to hold and help us. So near. He is longing for us to ask Him to make Himself real to us in our suffering. Somehow, He can turn our alone-ness into a sacred time through the glorious gift of His presence.

It blew my mind to ponder Isaiah 30, where we are told that our Creator waits for us so that He can show us compassion. It is an intense passage in which God is speaking sternly to the people of Israel, telling them that their choice to despise His words and instead believe lies will result in much calamity. But with the warning comes the antidote:

Only in returning to me and resting in me will you be saved. In quietness (stillness) and confidence is your strength. But you would have none of it. You said, 'No, we will get our help from Egypt. They will give us swift horses for riding into battle.' But the only swiftness you are going to see is the swiftness of your enemies chasing you! One of them will chase a thousand of you. Five of them will make all of you flee. You will be left like a lonely flagpole on a hill or a tattered banner on a distant mountain top. So the LORD <u>must wait for you to come to him</u> so he can show you his love and compassion. For the LORD is a faithful God. Blessed are those who wait for his help. (Isaiah 30:15-18, parentheses and underline added, NLT).

Often, we don't receive His help because we won't slow down or ask or wait. Let's begin to change that today. It's as simple as saying, "Here I am, Daddy. I am attempting to be still. Help me know that you are God. Amen."

I love the quote from Thomas Merton that is used in the book *The Lessons of St. Francis,* written by John Michael Talbot with Steve Rabey. "Not all men are called to be hermits, but all men need enough silence and solitude in their lives to enable the deep inner voice of their own true self to be heard at least occasionally."[23]

Talbot then declared the benefits he has learned through the practice of stillness. They are: "You know yourself better. You know God better. You know your purpose better."[24]

I wholeheartedly agree! It is well worth our time to invest in stillness.

This investment doesn't need to be one of hours and days. It can be a simple commitment of choosing to slow down our breathing and thinking for five minutes each night before we going to sleep, to just show up and say, "Daddy, I'm here. Have your way."

So, Beloved, let's learn from the Israelites' foolhardy ways and listen to what God is telling us. Let's allow Him to guide our steps throughout the day. In choosing to be quiet before Him, our hearts will lift in peaceful praise. We will be able to fly free amid the chaos with His strength and presence pacing us.

CHAPTER 10

Now, Not Cow

"..where the Spirit of the Lord is, there is freedom."
2 Corinthians 3:17

B ack in the day there was a saying: "Don't have a cow, man!" I think it originated with the television show *The Simpsons*[25]. It seemed like a condescending rebuttal after one received direction than a nice phrase; however, it makes me smile when I use it to my advantage now.

Taking the cow out of now is a necessary tool for combatting our freak-out tendencies. The "cow" is the freak-out, and the "now" is the gift.

Often, I find myself sabotaging my freedom by mentally leaving "now" and entering an imaginary scene for next week, next month, or even next year. On the surface, this may not seem like it's a big deal, but I have discovered that when I let my mind wander like this, I inevitably open myself to many triggers. Fear, doubt, insecurity, and worry have a heyday in the land of "Next time …."

As I begin to focus on the "possible" future, I let go of the present. I lose the ability to enjoy what is right before my eyes. The gifts God has given to me this day are shoved to the side, and for what? So that I can troubleshoot this or that possible scenario? Scenarios that will likely never happen occupy my mind, preventing me from flying free now. Instead chaos fills my mind, wasting my precious "now" on "maybes."

In a world of distractions where we have the ability to connect with many people instantaneously, our "now" is already congested. Technology is a double-edged sword of connectivity and chaos. How many of us remember the "olden days" when we had to literally pick up the phone and call one person at a time? Now, through numerous modes of social media, we can connect live and with ease.

I am not knocking technology and social media. They have their place and can be used for great good, but we also need to be aware of the harm they can bring. Distraction and the urgency for more can push us from the "now" into a fragmented mind-set that easily leads us to wasted time as we frantically try to stay connect with the many.

I mentioned in the last chapter how stillness can feel awkward, yet it is essential to practice so that we can fly free in the busyness of life. Taking time to be still is imperative if we are going to regain the gifts in this moment. Too often I've let go of my "now" and wished later I never had. The following entry from my blog[26], illustrates the point:

> There once was a hamster. She had never known anything other than her cage, and in it she was quite content. Her time would be spent between eating, drinking, sleeping, and watching those who would pass by her.
>
> One day she woke up to find something new in her cage. Unbeknownst to her, it was an exercise wheel. For days she simply stared at it and wondered what its purpose was. Eventually she ventured over to check it out

more closely. After a few weeks she became brave and finally discovered how to climb into the wheel and begin to walk. Slowly but surely, she began to really enjoy her wheel and found its entertainment was a fabulous way for her to spend the day.

Months went by, and the hamster became more enamored with her wheel. She simply had to be on it to feel alive and purposeful. She would set up challenges for herself to see how fast she could go. Life had never been better.

That is, until one bright sunny day when things got out of hand. The hamster got on her wheel and simply did not come off. She walked and then ran and then walked, ignoring her thirst, her tiredness, her hunger. Finally, when her body could not handle it anymore, she stumbled, and then came the THUD. Her beloved wheel had ejected her onto the floor of her cage......

I know the story could go on and be a lot more entertaining, but it's intended as a simple illustration God has used to help me keep myself and my priorities in check. I am that hamster, and the things in life that fulfill me make up the wheel. Water, food, and rest are the human necessities. The thud, well, the thud is what happens when the essentials are ignored. But I've been learning that there can be a self-inflicted thud that, although painful, is worth it.

In her book *21 Ways to Finding Peace and Happiness,*[27] world-renowned speaker, Joyce Meyer, writes very bluntly about how we alone oversee our schedule. Basically, what she says is quit whining and do something about it. I appreciate her bluntness because it is so refreshing, albeit painful, to be told directly what we can do to change. Needless to say, this reminder has been helpful in enforcing my "Thud Policy." We've all had that nagging feeling that tells us we should be done for the day, but instead we do "just one more thing." Or despite feeling yucky all day, we stay up that extra hour just because we can, only to feel just as gross the next day.

What I refer to as the "Thud Policy" is when I physically stop myself from continuing down the to do list and force myself to take a little break. It is REALLY hard to do, but I never regret the benefits. I especially need to enforce this policy when I am stressed out or having a busy week. The alternative is to keep running in hopes of not having to deal with my feelings or simply because it is weird to stop once I've been busy.

I find the "thud" uncomfortable because it usually means having to feel restless as I begin to slow down. But when I am still, laying with my eyes closed for a little bit, listening to the wind or music, it helps reset my rhythm, and I come back refreshed and refocused on what really matters.

Amid His busy time of ministry on earth, Jesus found time to be with His Father in solitude, and He encourages us to do the same. "Then Jesus said to them, 'Come to me, all of you who are weary and carry heavy burdens, and I will give you rest. Take my yoke upon you. Let me teach you, because I am humble and gentle at heart, and you will find rest for your souls. For my yoke is easy to bear, and the burden I give you is light.'" (Matthew 11:28-30, NLT).

This rest is ours for the taking. And when we choose to take time to rest in the "now," we lean away from "having a cow."

If our minds and plans are so far into the future that we are losing out on the present, then what is the point of our lives? I mean, how can we truly be doing what He has for us to do if we are not mentally involved in what we are doing? Taking time to be still is a way of reclaiming our "now." The following story from my blog[28] illustrates how we must be actively connecting to our Source to be able to live in the moment:

I was caught red handed.
Busted.
My hand stuck in the jar…
The jar of rotting manna.
"ROTTING MANNA?" you ask.
"Yep, rotting manna," I reply.

It's been a weird week. A week full of emotions about a variety of things. On Monday my head was like cotton balls at times, my spirit struggling with guilt and condemnation. Accusations attacked me as I drove to town even though I had my worship music cranked. The battle has been real, and I have just plain felt off my game. Like, OFF my game, like all the years of wrestling with fear and doubt hadn't happened and all the victories won over shame were a figment of my imagination.

I fretted, fussed, got angry, prayed, pleaded, apologized, and asked for prayer support from many. I tried to accept where I was at. I tried to remember God loves me where I am at. I tried to cram more truth into my head and heart, or up from my heart into my head, because I knew I'd been down this road numerous times before, and for some reason I just couldn't walk in victory. Everything within me felt off-kilter, along with a growing knowledge that I was again trying too hard.

So, I stopped and restarted, and then stopped and restarted until I was so exhausted, I just stopped. By then I was driving my beloveds to Awana and planning on spending time with our gorgeous daughter, but I was so drained. I knew I should be thankful for how they were all getting along, and I was, but in a numb, frustratingly unreal way. I turned on the tunes and listened to Lauren Daigle, trying to eat up every word of hope, life, and truth.

Slowly my spirit began to lift, and by the time Ally and I had had our treat and were heading back for the boys, my heart was joyful. I connected with some lovely souls at pick-up, and I was honest about my rough week. I received the gift of truth as I heard and began to believe again that we are all daily working through this and that and it's always only Him who can produce amazing things in us and through us.

Grace.

Wonderful, matchless, bountiful grace.

After a few days of searching, I went to bed feeling "found." I tried not to ponder where I had gone wrong, but I acknowledged that His grace had brought me back from the edge of deep discouragement and despair again.

Then this morning the pieces began to fall into place.

I had fallen for the self-sufficiency trap.

You know the one where you're starting something new, and you are scared, so you go back to the tried, tested, and true "things" that work: prayer, studying the Bible, listening, all of which are great disciplines. However, pride began surfacing as I believed, "I know what to do to get through this," instead of humbly saying, "Please help me, Daddy, it all feels so new."

My pile of plausible strategies looked great from the outside, but the rot my life was displaying told a different story. I started to create the plan for God: how He would save me, help me, and rescue me instead of waiting on God to fill me even in that very moment. I allowed myself to "live" five months into the future, imagining what things could look like instead of listening and breathing in the grace He's given me to do the steps He'd already taught me. I demanded more ability to believe instead of accepting my weakness. Rotten manna: demanding that past provisions work today instead of being dependent.

For those of you who have never heard of manna, it was bread that God supplied for His people when they were travelling through the desert. However, it came with strict instructions to only take a certain amount per day. If that rule was broken, the offender would wake up to rotten manna. In their attempt to be wiser than God, they would find themselves lacking in a way that would remind them in the future to trust Him.

Instead of holding my Daddy's hand and dancing in His grace, I constantly let go, demanding more of this and that to assuage my sins of pride, fear, worry, and doubt. Instead of accepting the Giver and basking in what He had already given me, I wanted more gifts, and now! My attitudes had been off--way off. And when I finally was drained by my efforts, I started to simply accept Him and what He was saying, which was just what He had offered me in the first place: Himself.

I'm so thankful I was caught trying to live off last week's victories. I'm so thankful my spirit remained unsettled to the point of distraction so that I would seek Him again and again until His gentle, steady grace enabled me not only to smell, but also to see that I was holding on to rotting manna. At that moment, the guilt I had been feeling melted away, and I had to smile at my foolishness and the beauty of how God works. He allowed me discomfort so that I would seek Him more deeply. He allowed me to be in community so I could share, listen, and hear truths I needed to be reminded of. He allowed me to feel the freedom of being like others who, like me, like all of us, daily battle with our vices.

I'm thankful that He reminded me that His way is fraught with deep peace and joy so that I couldn't be satisfied with the rotting manna.

You alone are the Way, the Truth and the Life, Jesus. Thank You for how You so gently busted me and brought me back to the abundant life of moment by moment walking with You.

The self-sufficiency trap is one we all fall into. But as we confess our mistakes to God and allow Him to forgive us and help us, we can always come back to freedom. He is the reason we can fly free, so we must slow down to receive what He has for us in this day, this moment. Our enemy would love for us to keep "having a cow," to see it as part of being human instead of the bondage it really is.

In the book *The Screwtape Letters*[29], C.S. Lewis writes about an older demon sharing what tricks his apprentice should use on humans. A piece of advice shared is that the human can connect with the enemy (God) in the present therefore, it is imperative that the human's focus be directed to the future. The devil's scheme is to have us dwell on the future to the point where we cannot enjoy the moment. I believe another trick of his is to have us forget about focusing on God in the moment. Do you ever wrestle with the fear that if you just focus on God in the "now," life will be boring? I have. What a trick of the Satan!

God designed us to live in the "now" with Him. God meets us in the present. What a beautiful thought! Our "now" is where we are connected to God and eternity. In the Bible, the book of Matthew speaks of the necessity to not worry about the future. Further on, James talks about how we have no way of knowing what will take place.

Let's choose to fight this freedom-killer that robs us of the gift of "now."

Let's combat it with the tools of stillness, self-control, and doing fewer things at one time.

Before writing this, I watched a webinar presentation by Kary Oberbrunner from Author Academy Elite. I was challenged by a quote in the presentation:

"Wherever you are, be all there." J. Elliot[30]

As we begin to practice this in our life, we will discover we are flying more frequently. Does the thought of not planning cause a huge struggle for you? Trust me, I get it. I am a planner! I have wrestled with God on this one, and through Sarah Young's devotional *Jesus Calling*[31], He challenged me to trust Him moment by moment, creating plans but choosing to hold them loosely.

The demons in *The Screwtape Letter*[32] concur with this theory and divisively attempt to push humans to focus on the possibilities of the future so that they are unaware of the gifts God gives them in the present. I say, "NO MORE! Satan, in the name of Jesus, leave us alone! We choose to enjoy now and all its beauty. We choose to enjoy our connection with our Source in this moment, praising Him for His help and presence. We choose to put down our phones, even turn them off, and focus--really focus--on the beauties that live in our home. We choose to not fear the future and what it may hold, but to revel in the NOW that God has given us. In the mighty name of the One who has given us now, Jesus!"

CHAPTER 11

The Peanut Gallery

"They lose nothing who gain Christ."
~Samuel Rutherford~

R emember how I wanted desperately to be a part of the "cool group" in elementary school? To me, they were the best dressed and most beautiful girls in our class. They had academic skills, athletic skills, and confidence. Did I mention their permed hair and amazing outfits?

I'd been bitten hard by the jealousy bug, and I so badly wanted to be like them. Everything about me seemed to be lacking: my confidence, my wardrobe, and my skills. I wasted a lot of time wishing to be in their group before finally discovering there were other amazing girls in my class that didn't fit the "cool group" criteria either. And I'm happy to say these "non-cool" ladies eventually became my bridesmaids. Well, let's just say we may not have been cool back in the day, but we are all beautiful now - on the inside and outside.

There are always opportunities in life to compare ourselves with others, and wow, when we do, we are basically handing that person chains to wrap us in. It's insecurity that causes us to want those in the cool group to recognize us. We think that if they do, that will somehow give us the validation we need to be special or important.

When we have a decision to make but are crippled by self-doubt because we are consumed by fear over what someone will think, or heaven forbid, say about us, the "peanut gallery" has come into play. I've discovered that others are actually thinking and talking about me way, way, WAY less then I think they are!

There are seasons in life in which insecurities shout extra loudly. At some point, I found I had to break up with my insecurities in order to fly free. I believe seasons of fatigue and change can trigger a lapse in our security. I know that when I try to find my security in what others think of me, I am always left feeling deflated and unable to receive enough compliments to have a lasting effect on me.

I will continue to wrestle with my mental peanut gallery, and that's annoying, but life on earth. Real freedom occurs when we choose the truth in a situation, even when wrestling. Let me share an example of victorious flying that took place at my kitchen sink:

> I am forming a habit of washing the "un-dishwasher-ables" in the morning after the kids go to school. Although I'm often tempted to skip, this time I didn't, as I'm beginning to realize it is a wonderful way to soothe my soul and think. I was in the process of refilling my cute counter-top pump bottle when I realized I was holding a nearly empty dish soap container. A grin started in my heart and worked its way up to my face as I put warm water in the bottle and squeezed.
> BUBBLES!!!!!

Beautiful, rainbow-filled bubbles, tiny and plentiful, soared above my sink.

I grinned at both my silliness and the freedom to be silly. I marveled at how glorious it was to play, even though there were no kids around. I reveled in the growth of my ability to be fully me in the moment, without the slightest qualm as to what I was doing or what others may think.

You and I both know these are victorious moments. It was so unlike the busy, exhausting season years before when I had four little kids at home and at any given moment often wondered what others were thinking about me. "What would so-and-so think if she knew I was laying down for a rest again?"

The pressure in my environment alone was plenty, then to add the internal pressure of measuring up to the assumed unspoken standards of others…yikes!!!! This is a definite recipe for freaking out! It was in that moment that I began to break up with my desire to please people who weren't even in my home.

Daily you and I make choices between living our life as our Source created us to or as we think so-and-so wants us to. Sometimes, like the other morning, my internal battle is intense.

"Oh man, the kids were up late. How tired, sore, and grumpy from sports will they be? How can I ….?"

My desire is to make them happy so my morning isn't tough. In trying to please them, however, I would be doing them a disservice. They need to learn how to cope with their triggers too, even if it makes my life tricky in that moment. This gives me the perfect opportunity to ask God for help as I teach them to acknowledge their triggers so they too can fly free. Do I really want to throw away this opportunity because I'm too tired?

I will always lean toward fixing the situation or making a decision that will leave others happy. Obviously, it's not wrong to take others into consideration, but allowing everyone else's opinion to direct our steps is a dangerous and sad way to live. We can't fly free when we are constantly ignoring ourselves.

In her book *Rising Strong*, Dr. Brené Brown[33] talks about the inner struggle. When we choose to wrestle with our natural response versus our unnatural but better response, we learn things about ourselves and situations that can lead us to amazing truth. But to reap the benefits, we must accept the challenge to engage in this un-fun battle.

Have you ever caught yourself saying, "Yes," when everything in you was screaming, "No," because you wanted the asker to be happy with you? Any given day provides countless opportunities for us to battle our tendency toward or away from people-pleasing.

What would it look like for you to lean away from people-pleasing?

For me it means remembering who my Boss is! I am in training to stop, ask, listen, and obey Him and His guidance on whatever situation I am facing. It means a lot of self-talk that goes something like this: "I am not responsible for everyone's happiness level. I am not in charge of others' actions or inactions. I am only in charge of my responses."

Lately, I've noticed that I am making choices that are truer to the me God created me to be, and with them comes a wild, fun-loving freedom. Have you ever watched other people go all-out at something, and maybe they didn't even nail it, but you were awed by them? Do you think it's because they didn't appear to care what others were thinking? They just went all-in and did what was in their hearts to do.

A huge motivator toward developing an all-in attitude regardless of outcome and what others think is knowing what God wants from us. This is why spending time with our Source and knowing how He views us is invaluable and vital to flying free. As I grow deeper in love with my Source and really believe His love for me is unending love, I am more willing and excited to trust and follow His lead. At times, His Holy Spirit reminds me with a check in my spirit that a freak-out is beginning if I choose to do this or that solely because so-and-so thinks I should... because what if?...

Removing "what if" and "I should because" from our vocabulary is a move worth making. When we exchange them for listening and believing our Creator and Source, we have a one-way ticket to flying free amid the chaos of the peanut gallery.

Acknowledging that we have a peanut gallery vying for our attention is a win. Being aware of the peanut gallery but pushing its persuasive voice aside to lean into our Source and follow His lead is what will send us flying! The choice is always ours. Will we let the "what if/you should" crowd continue to suffocate and dictate our steps, or will we lean into our Source and confidently hold His hand to fly free into the opportunities He has planned for us?

CHAPTER 12

Opportunities Prevail

*"The greatest freedom we have is to come right
to God at any time."*

~Anonymous~

The air was toasty warm, the sky a gentle blue. The water looked unending, the view breathtaking, as I snuggled more deeply into my lounger on the Dominican beach.

A sigh of contentment escaped, and a slight grin played on my lips when suddenly a shout shattered the silence. It was neither a panicked scream for help nor an impatient command but rather an exuberant invitation.

"Opportunity!" shouted the beach vendor. "Opportunity!"

My husband and I exchanged bemused grins as we enjoyed the unique twist to this vendor's marketing tactics. We did indeed have an opportunity to purchase his wares. Would we receive or reject this invitation?

We chose to reject what he was selling - a decorative ship, I believe. I regret not purchasing it or at least snapping a picture because that experience at the beach has forever changed my view on the word "opportunity." Had I known then that God would use the sound of that man's bellowing invitation regularly in my life, I would have purchased the ship as a daily reminder of my numerous opportunities to fly by faith with my Creator or freak-out on my own.

The hardest part about sharing this memory is that it's not possible to convey the volume of the voice that declared, "Opportunity!!!" To this day you may hear me buoyantly bellow, "Opportunity!" at the least expected times--like when the main course for dinner falls on the ground, or the tire is flat at the worst time imaginable. Shouting the word, "Opportunity!" has a way of making me grin or begrudgingly remember me that in any situation, I have an opportunity to trust my God or freak-out.

Granted, many of the opportunities we encounter are seldom what we had in mind. But we always, always, *always* are invited to take a step of dependence toward God in any decision or reaction to life we are making. When discerning our response, will we move toward or away from Him? We always get to choose.

For the record, moving toward Him is the way to go. God's way to deal with anything we go through in life always leads us to rise up and fly with Him through the chaos that threatens to drag us down. When we try to be God by trusting our own choices rather than Him, it causes us to struggle and eventually leads to freaking out in the chaos. Let's break it down into examples of physical, mental, emotional, and spiritual opportunities.

Physical:

I had been able to go to church, after which my family decided to go on a Sunday afternoon hike. I wanted to create this

FREAKING OUT TO FLYING FREE

memory with my children. This Sunday, however, my body loudly protested the proposed plan. There was no way it would be wise for me to go, so I made the painful but necessary choice to stay behind.

Opportunity came to call. No grin rose to my lips this time, however. Instead, as I realized I could release my family to go have fun without me or ask them to forfeit their plan for me, a tear rose to my eye. I could stay home, rant and rave over the injustice of a weak body, or I could be honest with my husband and my God about my frustration. God used this difficult opportunity to help me learn that instead of locking down emotion and forcing my body to keep going, I could listen to my body's need for rest and share my heart with my husband, which then also built intimacy. As I rested that afternoon, God brought me comfort.

This may not sound like flying free amid life's chaos to you, but for me it was. By yielding to God in a hard situation, I became free to enjoy Him in it, whereas freaking out that I didn't get to go on the hike would have simply created more chaos and exhaustion.

Emotional:

An onslaught of tears streamed down my face as I drove, brought on by memories, music, flashbacks, and a deep longing for my deceased big brother. The tears just simply would not stop. As I neared my destination, my anxiety increased. How could I shut these tears down? How would I get through my appointment without embarrassment? What if, heaven forbid, the receptionist was kind to me and asked about my day? I would end up weeping in front of her or even telling a lie to pretend I was ok. My mind was churning freak-out thoughts at the speed of the tires beneath me. What opportunity was there in this situation? Eventually I realized that becoming frantic beforehand would not help; what would be would be.

I did have an opportunity. I could trust that my God was with me and loved me whether I broke down in the appointment or not. I could believe that He would give me wisdom and grace to be vulnerable in a public setting or that He could stop my tears for a time and enable me to focus on my appointment. As it turned out the receptionist was kind and I was able to be honest and simply reply, "It's been a drippy day thus far."

This was a flying-free moment. I took the opportunity to trust God with the outcome, and in doing so, I was able to fly, unafraid of how the scenario would play out. The alternative would have been to cancel the appointment out of a fear of being vulnerable, and I would have missed the opportunity to fly free. The more often we choose to trust God when an opportunity arises, the more evidence we collect that He is who He says He is: faithful and good, always. He is enough!

Mental:

I am choosing a flop that turned into freedom for this example. My breathing was raspy. I clutched my throat and tugged at my collar. "Air, air, I need air," my mind demanded. The battle within raged loudly. "No, no, no! This isn't happening again - not now. I can't breathe. I can't breathe." Each frantic thought pushed me deeper into fear, closer to panic and terror.

"Stop!" I told the freaking out side of my brain. "You can breathe. You've made it through a thousand fatigue attacks. You will make it through this one. Yes, they suck, and yes, they are terrifying, but they never last forever. You are breathing; focus on breathing. In and out. Focus on Jesus. He is right here."

At a quick glance, it's easy to see this isn't a common mental battle, but the inner dialogue is what we do with ourselves every day. We always get to choose which thoughts we think and which thoughts we cut off. I know it may not seem like it, but we do. At any time, we can acknowledge whether the thought we are dwelling on is a part of the freak-out cycle or the flying-free cycle. We can then choose which cycle we want to be a part of.

A word to the wise: If we don't choose, it is highly probable that we will automatically end up freaking out. It's essential that we become aware of where our brains are leading us. We do get to control these thoughts, and by doing so decide which opportunity we are selecting.

In Part One, we investigated our triggers and modes of operation. As we remember our leans, we will be more aware of the moments of OPPORTUNITY. We always have a choice: trust ourselves or trust our Source.

Each opportunity seized to fly free can be a respite of hope and peace in an otherwise life-draining scenario. As individuals sick and tired of freaking out and determined to fly free, we will be under attack by God's enemy, Satan. He wants nothing more than to see us stay chained to the cycle of freaking out. He is always against us, and he knows how to activate our triggers.

However, we are not helpless and hopeless. Our Source is Almighty God, who is not afraid or remotely intimidated by Satan. In fact, God is the one who recognized that His angel, Lucifer, was wanting to become Him, which was absolutely impossible. God has always been, and He can never be replaced.

Consequently, Lucifer and his buddies were kicked out of heaven. Now the only way for them to get back at God for their banishment is to go after His kids. Satan tries to keep us in bondage in as many areas as he can, so we will never truly believe who our God is and how He has equipped us to fly free amid all circumstances --just like His Son Jesus did when He was on earth.

Hebrews 12:1b - 2a says, "Let us run with endurance the race that is set before us, looking to Jesus, the founder and perfecter of our faith." As we choose to seek God in every opportunity that comes our way, we can be sure we will begin to fly far more often than we freak-out. Opportunities abound, my friend --every single day! Will we choose to accept these opportunities as an invitation to fly, or will we flail about, freaking out and frustrated that nothing is going our way?

I encourage you to embrace your next opportunity as an invitation to trust the Source who knows all things and is always for you, never against you. Allow Him to open your eyes to what He has for you in whatever situation you are facing.

Is there something preventing you from accepting opportunities to trust God? If so, could your current mode of operation?

How is that working for you?

When is the last time you chose to trust God physically, mentally, emotionally?

What did that look like?

Was it worth it? Are you being completely honest?

Are you willing to start fresh this very moment by asking God to help you trust Him instead of freaking out the next time an opportunity arrives?

I pray you will, my friend, because viewing the challenges of life as an opportunity to trust our Source is a freedom-builder worth investing in.

In this section of the book we've talked about the importance of investing in developing our awareness of the freedom-killers out to get us. We've grown in believing the fact that God has provided a freedom-builder for every freedom-killer we encounter. Isn't that encouraging?! We are so utterly taken care of.

We have not discussed every freedom-killer or every freedom-builder, but as we begin to implement the framework in the next section, we will continue to build on the list of investments here. May our hearts begin to believe more deeply how much our God cares for us and that He always has what we need.

PART THREE

Implement

CHAPTER 13

Charge Up

"It is impossible to enslave mentally or socially a Bible-reading people. The principles of the Bible are the groundwork of human freedom."

-Horace Greely-

I sat in the corner of my laundry room, blurry eyed, trying to connect with my Source. It felt forced and empty. I put my head against the wall and cried. Only days before, my brother Byron had passed away. Emotions and exhaustion were so thick, I felt trapped, empty, and alone.

I'm an organized girl, so routine is not hard for me. I struggle more with the frustration and concern I feel when there seems to be a disconnect between us - when I feel I have shown up, but He is distant. I am growing in my remembering as Sarah Young shares in *Jesus Calling*[34], He is never the one to take a step away. All over Scripture, He states His committed love for us, despite our mess-ups.

I've discovered that distance often comes when somewhere along the line, I have stopped really talking to Him. I mean really talking - laying out my unfiltered feelings before Him. My walk with God has deepened as I realized I could express all my feelings to Him like the authors in the Psalms do. I now fully vent before Him without fear or guilt. "My victory and honor come from God alone. He is my refuge, a rock where no enemy can reach me. O my people, trust him at all times. Pour out your heart to him, for God is our refuge." (Psalm 62:7,8, NLT).

As I wept in the corner of my laundry room, I got real with God. I released my flood of sorrow, and He met me so tenderly, gently and fully.

It is my greatest desire that you would experience this tremendous love personally too. Get real with your Source. He can take it. He already knows and longs to let you feel His amazing grace again.

Do you ever feel like everything in life is interrupting your desire to connect with God? Maybe it goes something like this:

You purpose in your heart to wake up early for your personal time with God. The kids decide to get up a billion times that night. Somehow, you still manage to scrape yourself out of bed moments before "go time." With blurry eyes and a frustrated heart, you snag your Bible off the night stand and read some verses.

You already feel behind, and the day has just begun.

There are millions of ways and reasons our moments of solitude with God get interrupted. Sometimes we do sneak out of bed eager to be with our Daddy, our Source, only to discover one of the monkeys is up and wanting our attention.

Blocked goals are frustrating!!!

The blocked goal of having a devotional time can be heavier than others. Guilt gets involved, and our internal pressure grows. Desperation and frustration join forces, creating resentment and bitterness. We know we need this time. We know we can't control all the extenuating circumstances. In addition to all this, we face enemy attacks which make our goal of quality time with God even more difficult to achieve.

I have no magic formula that will suddenly make an uninterrupted devotional time appear for us, but I can say with certainty that God knows about our heart's desire and thwarted efforts. I believe He not only can, but He will open our eyes to various ways we can tweak our schedules, and even our expectations, of what we think our time with Him is "supposed" to look like.

For years, my devotions were done in a certain way: prayer list, read a chapter, maybe journal. Then when I finished what I'd planned to study, I'd be unable to decide what my next step was.

Life changes, seasons change, and we change. Don't be afraid to let go of your plan or to do your devotional time differently than usual. The purpose of time with God is - to spend focused time with Him, focused time on Him, remembering who He is.

Maybe it's time to just sit with Him on your favorite bench in the park or talk to Him during your daily commute or while making supper. Don't let your inability to do it perfectly keep you from trying at all. Maybe it's time to think differently - not as, "I have to," but instead, "Jesus, help me want to." And then ask, "What should our time look like today, Daddy? When should I pause to be with You? Please show me and help me obey. Thank you."

Our lives are full, but our days are His.

Will we allow Him to lead us to Himself?

Will we draw near to Him with a desire for Him to teach us who He really is?

Will we believe that He wants to share in our every day and will provide the opportunities for us to connect with Him?

There is no rule, "Thou shalt spend time with God daily." But in our heart of hearts, we all know that for us to get to know someone, we must connect with them. Here are a couple questions to help you start thinking about what works for you:

Where do you connect best with God? In nature? In your special chair? On a walk?

How do you best connect with God? By being quiet and listening? By reading the Bible and waiting? By studying a specific topic or word?

Throughout Scripture, God tells us He is willing to teach us. Are we willing to let Him do it His way? I pray that we are, "Oh God, grant us hearts that daily seek You. May we turn from guilt and shame toward believing and waiting in anticipation for what You have for us in each day. Amen."

Here are some Bible passages that testify to what we can enjoy as we spend time with our Maker.

The Lord says, 'I will guide you along the best pathway for your life. I will advise you and watch over you. Don't be like a senseless horse or mule that needs a bit and bridle to keep it under control.' (Psalm 32:8,9, NLT).

Joyful are people of integrity, who follow the instructions of the LORD. Joyful are those who obey his laws and search for him with all their hearts. They do not compromise with evil, and they walk only in his paths. You have charged us to keep your commandments carefully. Oh, that my actions would consistently reflect your decrees! Then I will not be ashamed when I compare my life with your commands. As I learn your righteous regulations, I will thank you by living as I should! I will obey your decrees. Please don't give up on me! (Psalm 119:1-8, NLT).

All the nations you made will come and bow before you, Lord; they will praise your holy name. For you are great and perform wonderful deeds. You alone are God. Teach me your ways, O LORD, that I may live according to your truth! Grant me purity of heart, so that I may honor you. With all my heart I will praise you, O Lord my God. I will give glory to your name forever, for your love for me is very great. You have rescued me from the depths of death. (Psalm 86:9-13, NLT).

But let the godly rejoice. Let them be glad in God's presence. Let them be filled with joy. Sing praises to God and to his name! Sing loud praises to him who rides the clouds. His name is the LORD–rejoice in his presence! Father of the fatherless, defender of widows– this is God, whose dwelling is holy. God places the lonely in families; he sets the prisoners free and gives them joy. But he makes the rebellious live in a sun-scorched land. (Psalm 68:3-6, NLT).

So humble yourselves before God. Resist the devil, and he will flee from you. Come close to God, and God will come close to you. Wash your hands, you sinners; purify your hearts, for your loyalty is divided between God and the world. Let there be tears for what you have done. Let there be sorrow and deep grief. Let there be sadness instead of laughter, and gloom instead of joy. Humble yourselves before the Lord, and he will lift you up in honor. (James 4:7-10, NLT).

But may all who search for you be filled with joy and gladness in You. May those who love your salvation repeatedly shout, 'The LORD is great!' (Psalm 40:16, NLT).

For us to break the habit of freaking out and experience the amazing adventure of flying free, time with our Source is imperative. I'd like to issue a challenge:

Would you be willing, just one time, to carve out 30 - 60 minutes to really talk to God and work through your feelings about Him?

Are you feeling resistance? Will you push into that resistance and ask for discernment as to why you are feeling this?

Is it possible you are angry with God?

We all have life stories, things we've gone through. I don't know what your experiences have been, but if you are angry with God, and the source of that rage is because those who called themselves His children have deeply wronged you, let me sincerely say, I am so very sorry.

Just like regular children, sometimes God's children do stupid and horrible things. I implore you to accept my challenge and allow yourself and God the opportunity to have a fresh start. I'm praying for you. Freedom is on the other side of this appointment. I so wish I could help you see His perfect love for you, but He alone can reveal Himself to you in a way that will resonate. After all, He is the One who designed you.

I'm not asking you to make this a daily commitment, but rather a restart appointment. Book a time where you can be alone, in a place you are free to write, rage, scream, yell, and weep if necessary. Bare your heart before Him, whatever it contains--whether it's joy, sorrow, rage, disappointment or unbelief. Once you've released it all, ask Him how the disconnect you are experiencing can be changed. Ask Him to open your eyes, heart, and mind to His truth. And ask Him to show you where and how you can take time in each day to be with Him. Then just sit and be still. Listen to your heart. Please do this, friends. Share your heart with the One who created you and loves you more than you could possibly love yourself or others. Lay everything out and give yourself a chance to start afresh with Him. You may need more than one of these all-out sessions with God before you are able to believe what He is saying to you. But my friend, this challenge is most definitely worth doing.

He is willing and waiting to daily interact with us. When we take the time to clear the air with Him, getting honest about all those aches and struggles, we are then able to sit back and let God minister to us. Clearly, He is invested in us since He was willing to send His only Son to die for us. But like any other relationship, things happen, and if we shove them down rather than dealing with them, the relationship cannot go forward.

If we let it all out and allow God to share His perspective and character, we can then release it all to His safe-keeping. Once our past concerns have been walked through with Him, we will be well on our way to realizing our daily need of connection with Him. Remember, He is the One who designed us (Psalm 139), the One who has called us to be His (Ephesians 1), the One who has equipped us to bear fruit for Him (John 15).

There are a myriad of ways to hang out with God, but some aspects remain the same. Depth with God is developed when we focus on Him and His character.

I read a profound book by Daniel Henderson called *Transforming Prayer*[35] that revealed to me the necessity of praying Scripture while focusing on what it said about who God is. Often, I don't hear how self-centered my devotion times are, but when they are, I don't feel as connected with God. When I choose to first surround myself in the truth of

His magnificence, I connect with Him in an amazing way. He is so patient and loving.

It is when we learn to focus on Him that our feet begin to leave our pile of earthly problems, and we begin to fly into His presence. And oh, what a sweet place it is. When we take time to focus on who God is, we begin to be thankful. As we are thankful, we become more honest with our God. Vulnerability brings about intimacy. Intimacy with Almighty God is empowering beyond our wildest dreams, enabling us to be at peace amid life's uncertainty and pain.

Here's the next challenge: Begin to ask God to show you when you are most aware of Him. Today I once again marveled at how I connect with Him as I fold laundry. My mind just started to declare the truth of who He is, and I began lifting up others to Him as I worked on my mundane task. I also love connecting with God outdoors. Nature has a way of drawing my thoughts to Him.

Sacred Pathways[36] by Gary Thomas is worthwhile reading to help you discover how you best connect with God. Nine spiritual temperaments are revealed by Gary enabling his readers to become aware of how they best related to their Maker.

It's okay to not know where you connect with God. Trust me, He will reveal it. "Draw near to God, and he will draw near to you." (James 4:8a, NLT).

Satan will try to discourage you, especially if you have any perfectionist tendencies. He will remind you that you don't even know how to connect with God, etc. God does not condemn those who seek Him. In fact, go to www.biblegateway.com and search the word "seek" to see God's generous and gracious response to those who earnestly seek Him.

Another way Satan tries to overwhelm or discourage is through confusion. We can become stuck wondering what or how to study. The Bible is a book of books, and it can feel tricky to read. However, it is worth it! There are so many resources available to help us if we want. More importantly, we have God's Holy Spirit. His actual job is to teach us (John 14:26). He is most definitely willing and ready to reveal Himself to us through the very book He created for us!

Sometimes it feels overwhelming to know where to begin studying or reading the Bible. It can be easier to read a devotional or join a small group study. These are great, but it is vital that you spend time alone with your Creator. He wants a real relationship with you. If you're starting out, but you're frozen in your perfectionism, kick it to the curb with truth. Tell yourself, "It is better to take the first step than to wait until I know how to do this perfectly. It's always about God's grace, never about my perfection. He is on my side in this. Therefore, I just need to start."

You could begin with this:

What book in the Bible intrigues you? Open it up and read. Jot down questions and thoughts that come to mind. Ask the Holy Spirit to open your eyes and heart to hear what He's speaking.

Does a specific phrase or concept stand out to you? Pause and write it down, and spend some time listening and asking God why this struck a chord with you. Maybe nothing is really jumping out at you. Don't worry, keep reading.

Ask God to show Himself to you through the passage you are reading. Then ask yourself, "How does this passage apply to me? What does this passage say about me?"

I've been studying the Bible for 33 years, and the bottom line is always this: Just show up to be with Him, and He will do the rest. Every time will be different. Don't worry about that. Just know that as you are obedient, God will be faithful. He will reveal Himself to those who seek Him.

I've found it's helpful to be aware of the unbelief points that have been a part of my thinking for years, then look in the Bible and see the truth. That way, when Satan stomps on a point again, I can refute him with truth.

Does this first step of the freedom framework seem impossible? Please, don't lose heart, my friend. When you choose to take this step--to just show up and tell God where you are at--He will meet you there. As you press on in this practice, it will feel less weird and more natural. Before you know it, you will begin to understand how vital charging up with your Source is in your transformation from freaking out to flying free.

We aren't quite finished yet. Before continuing, we have some action steps to take:

1. Make a "hash it out" appointment with God. Mark it on your calendar and respect this appointment. It matters!

2. Ask God when your daily time with Him should be. He may not whisper anything specific, but you might suddenly realize where time is being wasted and could instead be spent with Him. When is that? Where is that?

3. Choose what you will read, and then have a notebook and pen handy in whatever location you have as your meeting spot.

4. Begin to meet with Him, and continue.

5. Find someone you know who loves God. Share what you are learning and ask what he or she is learning.

Charging up with our Source is the power we need to implement the freedom framework He has provided. Just like our phones need to regularly be charged, we must also consistently charging up with our Source. Who better to turn to than the One who designed us?

CHAPTER 14

Own It

"You were chosen to be free."
~ Galatians 5:13~

Once we are charged up, we are more able to recognize when we are on the edge of freaking out. With our eyes on our Source and our hearts tuned into His Spirit, we will be more aware of when we're leaning toward a freak-out cycle. This is where we have opportunity to own it, which is our second step in the freedom framework.

Recognizing that we've been triggered creates a choice. We can pretend that is not where we are, or we can own it. Owning it means we are aware that a trigger's been activated, and in humility we bring this fact to our Source, asking for His help.

"Therefore, since we are surrounded by such a huge crowd of witnesses to the life of faith, let us strip off every weight that slows us down, especially the sin that so easily trips us up. And let us run with endurance the race God has set before us." (Hebrews 12:1, NLT).

I don't know about you, but it takes me some time before I am willing to acknowledge my "pet" sins, let alone throw them off. I'm learning to pray, "Please help me get sick and tired of the sins that entangle me so that I'm willing to throw them off."

I do get mad at myself for "blowing it" in words or attitude, but that's usually because my perfectionist side is miffed that her "perfect" score has been altered. This is then generally followed by the rationale that it wasn't entirely my fault. "If so-and-so had been more conscientious, then the event wouldn't have happened in the first place. In fact, if so-and-so would have done things my way, I could still be enjoying a guilt-free existence!"

I know none of you ever have that problem (wink, wink!), but this is the cycle I find myself in often. My reaction is sinful. I look for someone or something to blame. The entire process happens so fast, it's nearly instantaneous. I've become so skilled at rationalizing my sin that it's hard to stop and throw it off because, you know, "it really wasn't my fault."

I'm a blame-shifter. And this must stop. Changing this reaction can only be accomplished if I choose to depend on the Holy Spirit's help. As I choose to slow down and walk in step with Him, He will enable me to take responsibility for my actions or inactions. When I am obedient to His nudge that instructs me to turn from my selfish ways, then ask for forgiveness, I can move on and discern what I need to do to make amends. Sometimes though, believing I am forgiven can be sidelined by Satan's weapons of guilt and condemnation.

Often, when I choose to own that I have messed up, my performance anxiety reaches an all-time high; I get caught up in my perfectionism and become trapped at the "move on" part. I then have an opportunity to believe that God has forgiven me and to forgive myself as well, or I can get caught up in the performance anxiety trigger that will lead me to freaking out.

When I wrestle between believing I'm forgiven and performance anxiety, it can sound something like this: "I can't believe I acted that way again. I mean, I really knew better. Gee whiz, I've messed up the same way a bazillion times this very week. What is wrong with me?!! Why won't I change?" The tangles of sin now begin to strangle me as I wrap myself in its chains of condemnation and unbelief.

Hang tight, friends. There is good news!

I can grow by calling my sin, sin.

I can acknowledge it for what it is and resist my tendency to strangle myself by accepting God's epic grace again and again.

I can cut off the sin that is trying to hold me fast.

Granted, for any of this, I need God's help. To cut off anything...well it hurts. It also hurts to acknowledge that the unease I'm feeling is my conscience agreeing with the Holy Spirit that the remark I made was thoughtless and requires an apology. There is resistance against feeling the sting of the consequence for my sin. In order to avoid that sting, I can let resistance control me and allow myself to stay on the path towards freaking out or I can choose to push into the resistance, receive true forgiveness and restoration, and be well on my way to applying the next step of the freedom framework.

I am learning to face the resistance and ask myself this question: "What am I trying to hold onto in this situation?"

Often the answer is my pride!

As I recognize that my resistance to the pain of confession is rooted in sin, I'm much more motivated to go through that confession. The pain then becomes part of my victory as I repeatedly choose to repent and turn from the sin that has been controlling me. The victory of throwing off my sin brings the joy and confidence that I can walk unfettered because I can, with His help, become untangled and continue.

As I've contemplated writing about this challenge, it became obvious that it's not all about sin. In fact, the Bible verses that talk about throwing off sin always connect to the mighty work of Jesus Christ (Hebrews 12:1,2). I recently heard a wise saying: "Don't be so focused on your sin, but on the One who cleanses you from it."

So dear ones, why don't we pause right now and ask the Holy Spirit to make us aware of our pet sins and to give us the desire to own them when they surface so that we can truly be set free from their hold? Not only is He willing to point out when we are being tangled up by temptation and sin, He also promises to always provide a way out. First Corinthians 10:13 says, "The temptations in your life are no different from what others experience. And God is faithful. He will not allow the temptation to be more than you can stand. When you are tempted, he will show you a way out so that you can endure." (NLT).

When we mess up and don't take the way out that He offers, He is willing to forgive us as we own that we need His cleansing.

The Scripture below testifies to His willingness to cleanse us:

> Therefore, since we are surrounded by so great a cloud of witnesses, let us also lay aside every weight, and sin which clings so closely, and let us run with endurance the race that is set before us, looking to Jesus, the founder and perfecter of our faith, who for the joy that was set before him endured the cross, despising the shame, and is seated at the right hand of the throne of God. (Hebrews 12:1,2).

> There is therefore now no condemnation for those who are in Christ Jesus. For the law of the Spirit of life has set you free in Christ Jesus from the law of sin and death. For God has done what the law, weakened by the flesh,

could not do. By sending his own Son in the likeness of sinful flesh and for sin, he condemned sin in the flesh, in order that the righteous requirements of the law may be fulfilled in us, who walk not according to the flesh but according to the Spirit. (Romans 8:1-4).

This is the message we have heard from him and proclaim to you, that God is light, and in him is no darkness at all. If we say we have fellowship with him while we walk in darkness, we lie and do not practice the truth. But if we walk in the light, as he is in the light, we have fellowship with one another, and the blood of Jesus his Son cleanses us from all sin. If we say we have no sin, we deceive ourselves, and the truth is not in us. If we confess our sins, he is faithful and just to forgive us our sins and to cleanse us from all unrighteousness. If we say we have not sinned, we make him a liar, and his word is not in us. (1 John 1:5-10).

When we feel our temperature rising, as every household member seems to be ignoring the call to dinner, owning it will help us move away from freaking out. When we are triggered, we can own it by choosing to pause and connect with our Source, asking for His forgiveness for being quick to anger and for His help and wisdom to know how to handle that specific situation.

Sometimes owning our actions sounds like, "Oh sorry, I was jumping ahead of what you were saying instead of really listening. Could you start again, and I'll pay attention this time?" When we own that we are about to blow it, we redirect and turn away from freaking out to flying free. The beauty of owning it is that it can happen at any place--pre-freak-out, mid-freak-out, or post-freak-out--and it always positions us to fly free.

In her book *Rising Strong*[37], Dr. Brené Brown talks about the power of owning our mess-ups, discovering their root and then applying a change to continue forward growth. Owning where we are at, then delving into how and why we got there will bring us to step three of the freedom framework.

CHAPTER 15

Discern It

*"But the Scriptures declare that we are all prisoners of sin,
so we receive God's promises of freedom only
by believing in Jesus Christ."*

(Galatians 3:22, NLT)

The feeling of dread was dark and deep. The thoughts that swirled through my mind began mostly with, "What if?" and "I can't," with a lot of "How???" sprinkled in. "I don't know how I'll survive once he dies," I blurted out to my friend.

After fighting cancer for five years, it seemed my oldest brother, Byron, was in his last days on earth. I'd received the information and was deciding if/when I should book a flight for what may be my last time with him. If possible, I knew I wanted and needed to see him again while he was alive. I also knew I needed to process these heart-wrenching moments with my good friend. We both knew that I would never regret going, so I needed to.

As the intense fear of how I'd survive after By left earth began to come up, with deep grief surrounding every word, my sweet friend calmly but firmly redirected me. "Andrea, we aren't doing that right now."

She was right. My focus needed to shift from the future to now. Right now, I had an opportunity, and I needed to focus on the steps necessary for me to be by Byron's bedside sooner rather than later.

Simply put, discernment is getting to the bottom line of the issue at hand. Once we've owned that we are near or in a freak-out, we need to discern why so that we can redirect to freedom. In the above situation, freedom was spending my energy in preparation for the trip instead of stressing about the future.

Discernment is our third step in the freedom framework.

Pausing to acknowledge when a trigger has gone off is wisdom. In the case above, the trigger was terror of the future, or handling something that had never been handled before. It was not the right time to walk through either scenario, though. I needed to stop focusing on my fears or I would have freaked out deeply. These were normal and natural reactions to the information I was processing, but had I lingered there, I may have missed my opportunity to make the decision and act in a time-sensitive situation. With my friend's help, I was able to discern this unhelpful deviation and get refocused on the present.

This may not sound like flying free to you, but it was, in the sense that my friend and God refocused me on the now and reminded me that God would enable me to survive the future too.

Thankfully, everyday examples are less intense, yet each time we face a trigger, we will experience some resistance.

In the last chapter, we mentioned how it hurts to acknowledge we've messed up. It also hurts, or even angers us, to acknowledge when a trigger is winning again. At least, that is what it can feel like. Of course, this is also the enemy of our soul trying to sabotage us with our already raw emotions, telling us that it's not possible to change our path. In fact, it's highly probable as you've been reading this book that you've wrestled with picking it up and continuing. It's challenging to take responsibility and to act differently than we have in the past. I'm proud of you for sticking with me this far. You know what I am going to say: This is hard, but it will be worth it. I promise!

Discernment is choosing to push through the resistance while honestly questioning, "Why?" so that truth will be revealed. Once that truth is revealed, we are given a choice. The choice we make will either set us free or lead us to freak-out.

An everyday example of this is when I realize that I am being short-tempered with my family. I can keep going down that road and blame them for my reaction, or I can own it and ask God for insight into the "why" behind my reaction. Granted, pausing and humbling myself to ask God for discernment is HARD! My go-to is to try to out-run my problem, but that just makes things worse faster. Stopping and asking is by far the better choice, holding tremendous value. We've charged up and owned up to the fact that our triggers have gone off. Now we choose to pause. We defeat resistance by asking our Source to help us discern the "why" to our response.

Just the other day I found myself going through these steps, only to discover my angst toward my husband was because I was expecting him to be like God to me. The poor guy didn't stand a chance against my unrealistic expectation!

I am so glad I paused to discern what really set me off. Once I was able to see my unrealistic expectation for what it was, I could then choose to trust God to provide all that I needed. And He did.

In order to receive discernment from God, we need to slow down and take a minute to connect with Him. This can be as easy as excusing ourselves to another room, and it may sound something like this: "Ok, Jesus, I'm stopping. Why am I responding this way to the kids? Please open my eyes and heart to the root of this."

I find that as I pause and listen, thoughts float through my mind, usually landing on my "why." I believe often we will eventually, or sometimes easily, realize it's because we are feeling tired, behind, taken advantage of, or unheard.

Once we are aware of the "why" behind our behavior, we then have an opportunity to flesh it out more fully. And that may sound like this:

"I am tired. I need help, Daddy. You promise to be my strength. Please calm my heart and help me react out of love because of Your Spirit. If there is a solution to my fatigue, help me have the courage to implement it. I feel scared that laying down for 15 minutes will make me fall behind. Please help me trust You and obey."

The discernment process is tricky to implement because of needing to pause, but it's imperative. If we do not stop to own our triggers, and then connect with our Source for discernment, quite simply, we will stay on the path that leads toward freaking out.

Freaking out does not need to be a fact we accept. We have our Maker and Provider waiting to help us. All we need to do is pause, ask, and take the action step He reveals.

Discerning our "why" will lead us to the question, "What can I do about this situation?" thereby providing us with an action step. We can trust that our Source considers this step an opportunity to reconnect with Him. He will reveal which freedom-stealer has taken the upper hand and remind us of the freedom-builder He provides to counter it.

When in the discerning stage, some of the questions we can ask ourselves are:

Am I operating out of grace or legalism?

Am I wondering what others will think?

Am I acting out of my identity in Christ or something else?

Am I believing God is who He says He is? If not, why not?

What truth about God and His view of me have I ditched in this moment?

A roadblock to any of these framework steps is a simple unwillingness to do what we know we need to do. When this happens, we are choosing to STAY on the path of freaking out.

Here's a personal example:

My body is exhausted. My anxiety is maxed, knowing that I am heading for a fatigue attack. I start trying to accomplish more things while desperately wanting someone to acknowledge where I'm at, recognize my work, and tell me to stop. Instead of doing this for myself I allow fear to continue bullying me. It whispers debilitating words into my heart: "Get it all done. You don't know how long you'll be down for this time. Hurry!!! Think of all the work that will be left for your poor hub and the kids if you don't do it!!"

Its lies touch my heart. And as I urge my weary limbs to continue, a seed of resentment is watered, and I hear myself snap at the kids, the same ones I am supposedly conquering the world for. Eventually my husband gives me an odd look and gently suggests I go lay down.

"No," I snarl, even as my head spins and my legs wobble because now I'm mad at him for not saying something sooner. He should have been more aware of me and how I was doing! I try to fight through my physical weakness by pushing myself harder rather than listening to its pleas for back-up. Instead

ANDREA FEHR

of discerning that in the end, slowing down would be better, I allow my fear-filled thinking to lead me to this place.

With my fatigue on the verge of eruption, I eventually remove myself from the supper table. I lay down, feeling foolish, defeated, and angry that any of this happened at all. Once in bed, I have time to discern what happened.

I knew I was exhausted, BUT I chose to continue because of anger at my chronic illness. I listened to pride declaring that, "This disease will not control me!" I allowed fear free reign to bully me by saying, "How long will you be out for this time?"

Each of these emotions had a legitimate place in my experience, however allowing them to dictate my actions was foolishness. Pausing for discernment would have brought me to that place where I allowed God to comfort my fears and anger, where He would help me humble myself to trust Him and His ways, where I'd rest a little. In all likelihood, doing so would have minimized, or possibly nullified, my fatigue attack.

I've said it before, and I will say it again: This step is hard, BUT it is worth it!

As we continue to practice, we will begin to see which lies about God and ourselves we most readily run to when a trigger is hit. Once that happens, we can spend our charging-up time finding specific verses to combat those lies. When we grow in our ability to pause and discern, we will inevitably run more often to our Source--the One who is always willing and wanting to participate with us in whatever challenges we are facing.

Discernment slows us down to reconnect with our Source--the One who is all-knowing and fully able to help us in our moment of struggle. He has equipped us, but it's up to us to believe what He says about us, and then trust that He will help us walk it out.

One spring, I was feeling extreme internal pressure about my home business. Even though I'd just started out, I was

124

really feeling the pressure to earn money. Obviously earning money is a normal goal for a business, but I knew the pressure in my gut was louder than necessary. Something was off.

I asked myself the "why" of the emotions, and with God's help, I was able to discern that I was operating partially out of the fear that I needed to grow my business large enough to sustain our family. This was not based on any real need, only on the fear that one day I may need to, and I doubted that I would be able to. With God's help, I was able to get to the root of my fear-based pressure and replace it with truth. God hadn't called me to be the main source of income in our family. God has always provided for us, and He always will. Freedom and peace returned as I discerned where my thinking and feelings had led me astray and allowed God to lead me back to His truth.

The beautiful thing about this discernment session is that it took place on a bench in an arena where I was waiting for an event to begin. Don't be deceived into thinking one must spend hours discerning each situation. It really just takes a few minutes to apply the steps we have talked about. We connect with our Source by owning it when we are headed toward a freak-out. We ask Him for discernment. As He supplies it, He helps us determine our action step, and we are well on our way to victory!

Let's take some time to evaluate:

What are you regularly feeling in your life?

In what area are you leaning toward a freak-out? Ask yourself, "Why?"

Why is this issue stirring up panic in me?

What am I forgetting about God, His character, and His promises?

What has this way of thinking gotten me so far?

What will I choose to believe?

As we commit to practicing this step of discernment, we are on our way to victory. Victory is where we will begin to walk out the action step God has revealed. When we do, we will be on our way to flying in freedom.

CHAPTER 16

Victory!!!

"If you want to be free, just start doing what
God wants you to do."

~Joyce Meyer~

"I do believe I'm walking away with the victory!" (Third Day[38]). Victory! Arms in the air, a huge grin spreading across your face, jumping up and down, giving high fives to random strangers, cheers of joy filling the air--this is the mental picture that may arise when we hear the word victory. This is what victory looks like at a stadium.

Victory!!!! It feels like there is so much joy rolling around inside, you simply have to shout or dance to celebrate what has just taken place. Victory feels like elation, contentment, and hope all rolled into one.

I love the word victory--so much so that I need to actively choose not to type it in all capitals with multiple exclamation marks! The word victory is a powerful word.

Somewhere along this road of life, I decided that my relationship with God would have me feeling victorious all the time. This unrealistic expectation often left me feeling behind and defeated in my walk with God instead. As my perfectionistic, melancholy tendencies kicked holes in my sanguine dream of a Christian life full of victory, I struggled, wondering if victorious living was just a myth rather than a practical reality. It's because of this wrestling that I began learning to fly free.

Sunday school songs like, "I'm inside, outside, upside, downside happy all the time. I'm inside, outside, upside, downside happy all the time. Since Jesus entered in and washed away my sin. I'm inside, outside, upside, downside happy all the time,"[39] didn't help my young literal mind. I wasn't always happy.

Was being happy victory? What was victory? Why did Christians proclaim they had it in song, but clearly did not live it in their day-to-day?

While growing in acceptance of God's grace, I challenged these incongruencies, and my warped perception of victory changed.

My new definition of victory was formed through the book titled *Jesus Calling*[40] by Sarah Young. This new description of victory was simply "connecting with God."

WOW!

My whole "trying too hard" system was so unnecessary. My victory is found from simply connecting with God. This means just showing up, just saying a prayer or a sentence of thanksgiving, or just being still with Him.

As I began believing this truth, I was able to celebrate each time I turned to God in my day. Before I knew it, I realized I was flying in freedom. By focusing on my Source, the chaos lost its strength to ground me. And as I focused on my Source amid life's drama, I found myself refreshed and encouraged. I was able to beam at those around me even though my prayers were in waiting because I was trusting the One who knows all things.

Life is no longer about me trying to fix things. It's not about doing this or that plan. It's about daily releasing myself into His hands. Victory is letting the Source of our life lead us.

As we charge up, then own it and confess where we've gone off track, we can discern what went wrong and what needs to change. And then comes the beauty, the magic, if you will.

I know it sounds hokey, and honestly it can feel hokey, but I am telling you as we apply the freedom framework, we will see results. To get to that place where our hearts are bursting with praise is so worth the beginning awkward moments. As we implement the steps of the freedom framework, our perspective is changed. Before we know it, we are at peace even though the chaos around may not have altered at all.

I hesitated to call this book *Freaking out to Flying Free* because I was concerned that you, my reader, may think that I was implying that I never freak out anymore, when in fact, I must choose every day, multiple times a day, to fly free. It may be disheartening to hear that we will daily battle between freaking out or flying free, but as the freedom framework steps are applied, we begin to fly more often, and we feel empowered to fight the cosmic battle that we are a part of. I had to accept the fact that I'd been wasting energy being annoyed at the battle, and then choose instead to spend that energy in applying God's principles for freedom.

Victory is ours when we realize we have a daily Savior.

It may be painful to accept that we are weak, but we have only ever been the ones under the illusion that we are supposed to be strong. Our weakness is a gift He gives. The result of our weakness is dependence on God, and that is what draws us back to Him.

From his book *Eve*[41], William P. Young's rendition of what
an angel's reaction to the creation of man may have looked
like was comical because the angel was shocked by how helpless and inconsequential humans appeared. This is how I feel
often - fragile, weak, and inconsequential, but Creator God's
response in the book lines up with what He says in Scripture
as He declared us that it is not possible to understand His
unending love for us, His creation.

Wow! We cannot drift out of His unending love!

I remember years ago, at the start of our church's Vacation
Bible School week, I felt upset and frustrated, fragile and weak.
As I burst into one of the classrooms to vent to a friend, I
realized that my job for the evening was to teach the kids a
memory verse. There on the wall was a cheerful poster of the
verse that seemed to mock my tortured soul.

"I praise you, for I am fearfully and wonderfully made.
Wonderful are Your works; my soul knows it very well.."
(Psalm 139:14).

I was incredulous! Was I really supposed to teach this verse
when I was despising myself?

I was. And it was a powerful moment of realization. Who I
am and what I may be feeling can be two very different things,
BUT I always have the choice to believe what God and His
word say about me or carry on rejecting Him and His truth.

Trust me, in order to believe that verse and have my heart
and mind changed, I needed some serious help from above.
But it was, and continues to be, worth it.

Will you lean into the truth of what God says of you in
His Word, the Bible? He has created us to be vulnerable; this
wasn't part of the curse. This is a gift, so that we will drink
deeply of Him always because He is the only true source of
Life and freedom.

Will you ask Him to help you praise God for how you are
fearfully and wonderfully made? Ask Him to help you declare
yourself wonderful. How would doing this change the way

you think and talk to or about yourself? How could shifting toward acceptance of your weakness change your relationships with others?

From time to time, we all need the reminder to love ourselves because God loves us. If we allow ourselves to believe God's unending love for us, we will begin to be at peace with our fragility and weakness. We can become okay with our naked need for Him. He created us naked and unashamed. We don't need to hate what we look like or who we are. It does not bless Him to hear us hate on ourselves. We have an opportunity to believe that being vulnerable before God, without shame, is always how He intended for us to be. Let's take a moment and ask Him to heal our wrong thinking and embrace who He's called us to be--body, soul, and mind.

Our dependency, weakness, and fragility are gifts that can draw us to Him daily, even hourly, if we let them, or they can cause us to turn from Him to try to be something we were never created to be: invincible and self-sufficient.

Friend, I have tried both ways, and naked and unashamed wins hands-down! Being able to depend on my all-knowing, all-sufficient, perfect Father of Light is freeing, and it can even be fun as I learn to wait for Him to lead, guide, fix, and solve all the ups and downs of life.

So the next time you feel fragile and weak and are tempted to fight it by trying harder, would you do yourself a favor and smirk a little as you declare, "I am naked and unashamed. I am fragile and weak, but this is exactly how God created me to be. It is not wrong to need God. He created me this way. Needing Him is a gift that allows me to fully enjoy my Source of life and freedom in every moment. Here I am, Daddy. Please help me. Thank you."

You'll be amazed how this change in thinking will bring you peace and joy.

Here are some verses about our loving Creator and his view of us:

> What sorrow awaits those who argue with their Creator. Does a clay pot argue with its maker? Does the clay dispute with the one who shapes it, saying, 'Stop, you're doing it wrong!'......This is what the LORD says--the Holy One of Israel and your Creator: 'Do you question what I do for my children? Do you give me orders about the work of my hands? I am the one who made earth and created people to live on it.' (Isaiah 45:9a,11,12, NLT).

> Even before he made the world, God loved us and chose us in Christ to be holy and without fault in his eyes. God decided in advance to adopt us into his own family by bringing us to himself through Jesus Christ. This is what he wanted to do, and it gave him great pleasure. So we praise God for the glorious grace has poured out on us who belong to his dear Son. He is so rich in kindness and grace that he purchased our freedom with the blood of his Son and forgave our sins. He has showered his kindness on us, along with all wisdom and understanding. (Ephesians 1:4-8, NLT).

Please don't let your misled thinking and fickle feelings keep you from deep soul-healing and freedom. Freedom comes from knowing we're created by God with a love that doesn't end--the same love that doesn't expect us to know it all and allows us to be naked and unashamed.

Acknowledging our need for Him is victory. Believing what He says is victory. Refocusing on Him and who He is, is victory. Instead of keeping track of our mess-ups, let's start cheering for ourselves when, at any given moment, we choose to fly by working through the freedom framework.

Having a mode of operation that doesn't lead to freedom is part of being human. However, we do get to choose which mode of operation we will use. I am trading mine of fear, doubt, pride and control for faith, confidence, and humble dependence on Almighty God. What will you choose?

Here is God's promise to us through Jesus:

Jesus said to the people who believe in Him, 'You are truly my disciples if you remain faithful to my teachings. And you WILL know the truth, and the truth will set you free.'

'But we are descendants of Abraham,' they said. 'We have never been slaves to anyone. What do you mean, 'You will be set free'?

Jesus replied, 'I tell you the truth, everyone who sins is a slave to sin. A slave is not a permanent member of the family, but a son is part of the family forever. So if the Son sets you free, you are truly free.' (John 8:31-36, NLT, emphasis mine).

Will you join me, and choose to live it today?

Together, let's choose to walk out His truth until we sense that we are flying amid the chaos of our lives. Let's celebrate every time we do any step in the framework, acknowledging that freedom is His design for us. Let's rise up together and walk diligently through the framework, so when those around us see the changes in us, they'll ask, "How?" and begin their own journey toward freedom.

As we daily apply the freedom framework- charge up, own it, discern it - we are led into VICTORY!!!

VICTORY is turning to our Source and His freedom-builders in any situation we face!!! Beautiful Warriors, rise up with me, embrace the freedom framework God created, so that daily we can fly free!!!

PART FOUR

Impact

CHAPTER 17

The Game Changer

"We are in love
We are in freedom
We are in hope for we are in Jesus."

~Anonymous~

F riends, you've come this far. Good for you!!! You've bought the book with the radical title because you had a desire, a yearning, to fly free amid life's chaos.

We've investigated our triggers and modes of operation. We have become aware of the freedom-killers and builders that lead to victory. We have learned the freedom framework and understand the steps within it. We are aware of how living a life of freedom will benefit our body, soul, and mind, and, by extension, others. Now it's our responsibility to begin acting on all we have learned. We were made to soar in life through trusting our Creator. We were created to glorify Him by deeply enjoying His presence, allowing Him to alleviate our cares and concerns in this crazy world.

We live in a world where there is so much pain and suffering, so much disillusionment about who or what our source should be. There are numerous opinions regarding how much freedom we can really have. Cynics, critics, skeptics, realists, and pessimists vie for our attention, while dreamers, motivators, and positive thinkers try to sway us in a different direction.

I can't protect you from that struggle, but I can assure you that implementing the tools we have discussed has changed my life and I will never look back.

Freedom is facing the chaos within us and our lives alongside our everyday Savior.

Freedom is knowing our Source, Jesus, is always enough.

Freedom is waking up with our souls filled with worship.

Freedom is going to bed at peace, knowing we don't need to conquer the world.

Freedom is having our security and confidence in our God, not in the peanut gallery.

Freedom is being released from our internal struggles, so we can see others and encourage them towards our Source.

As I repeatedly apply the freedom framework in my own life, I find myself growing in my ability to consistently experience victorious living. My body, mind, and soul are freed and available to connect with my Jesus at any given moment. I am far more aware of His presence and my need for Him throughout my day. I have a heightened sense and perspective of Him in my life, and I glow with His joy and love. My time is productive and fulfilling, spent on joy-filled living instead of drowning with internal struggle. I feel confident and equipped to acknowledge the struggle and respond appropriately through the freedom framework, which then brings me back to dancing in adoration and praise of my good God.

I have found the triggers that were once so very loud and powerful have lost much of their power. I am growing in the life-changing awareness that I have everything I need to do God's will. Satan attempts to defeat me by whispering discouraging words into my heart--a lie that sounds something like, "Wow, you have to go through the freedom framework again?!?"

The truth is, on this side of Heaven, I will always wrestle with my triggers, but defeat only comes with allowing them to control me instead of using the tools God has given me to enjoy the freedom He provides.

Flying free often involves effort, but it's always worth it when we leave the chaos behind and begin to fly.

I love that God has opened my eyes to the freedom framework He's been growing in me for years. I am honored to be able to model it for my family and friends and share it with all who are ready for an action plan that will change their lives. I love that as I'm out-and-about in life, I can see the needs of others because my soul is free to be in the moment, fully enjoying my God, aware of His nudges to interact with others.

What a gift we give the world when we implement the freedom framework and regularly fly free! When we are flying amid the chaos of this world, so many are impacted. It's true we don't fit in as well when we aren't willing to continue the cycle of freak-out in life, but it's important to know that our example gives hope to others. It is a powerful and beautiful thing to live in the freedom, peace, and joy that God has provided for us. I've noticed that people seem drawn to me, and all I'm doing is living life with my heart turned toward God.

At a reception after my Grandpa's funeral, I sat with a beautiful senior soul. My soul was at peace and in awe as I visited with her. I knew that she'd been through an enormous amount of tremendous difficulty in her life, yet her countenance was radiant, and joy beamed from her being. Finally, I just asked her what made her glow. Swiftly and simply, she replied, "Jesus."

Dear Friends,

We are all given the choice whether to go deeper in our relationship with Jesus or not. Will we believe that He died to give us abundant life, to make our joy in Him overflow, as He says in His Word? Or will we choose instead to rationalize that we don't really freak-out that much, and we don't have that much stress in our life? We can sabotage our earthly lives when we say we believe in God and are friends with Him, but we never actually allow Him into the deep places within to work in a life-changing way.

By now you know which way I have chosen, and nothing in the world will change my choice to live in the freedom and joy He died to provide.

Won't you join me?

Purpose in your heart to charge up with your Source so you can fly through life's joys and sorrows with a deep knowledge that He's got you and your situation. I pray that if you haven't already, today you will make the commitment to replace freaking out with flying free. I promise it is not only possible, it is incredible, and it will powerfully impact you and those around you.

CONCLUSION

Inspire

Inspire

*"This is your year for freedom.
Your year of breakthrough.
Your year of Jubilee."*
-Anonymous-

You know by now that I believe that breaking free from our freak-out cycle and learning to fly free is a choice--one that it is absolutely possible! I have been honest in sharing that it will take work to change, but I've also repeatedly said that it will be worth it. It's the daily choices we make, one after another, that determine if we will fly. I don't know about you, but to me, flying sounds much more amazing than the awkward, painful consequences that come with choosing to freak-out.

We all know that the thought of flying free is powerful, inspirational, and moving. We are each equipped to fly free. We have what we need to succeed. Will we choose to do it?

I pray that in the pages of this book you have found a motivation beyond your wildest dreams to break your old patterns and discover freedom in every stressed-out area of your life, that your desire to grow will be so loud that you

143

willingly surrender your chaos to His freedom framework, so you can fly free. I pray you'll have a heightened awareness of both your triggers and modes of operation, and that this awareness will mobilize you to act on what you have learned. I pray that your Warrior within will become furious at the enemy for holding you back through destructive lies and that you will be fueled to press through the work, awkward moments, and failures, to seize this opportunity and fly free amid the chaos of life.

You CAN do this, friends!!! Your Creator has made you for this moment - to fly free, fueled by His unending love for you! Go fly, my friends, in freedom, grace, and truth! And as you do, people will be drawn to you and to your Source. You will have the hope to give to those who feel hopeless. You will have opportunities to share how your life has been changed. You will become radiant as you trust your Source with all the chaos in your life. He will produce beautiful things in and through you: solid relationships, opportunities to mentor, joy for others.

Become aware of your need for Him and His incredible provision for you through His grace and forgiveness! Accept the victorious and abundant life that is yours for the taking by staying close to Him! Thank Him for how He has created you to fly and for how it will affect your relationships at home and beyond!

Go inspire the world by FLYING FREE!!!

Dear Reader,

I am so proud of you for choosing to read my book. I trust you are excited and motivated to apply freedom builders to your life.

I wanted to let you know that I do offer personal and small group coaching for those who would like to process their discoveries further.

Coaching is a beautiful and sacred place where individuals gain: clarity, accountability and relationships that help them implement what they have been learning about.

If this resonates with you, please connect with me at www. andreafehr.com

I would be honored to journey with you further.

Sincerely your sister in Christ,
Andrea Fehr

Endnotes

Introduction

1. Wilkinson, Bruce. *The Prayer of Jabez*. Chicago, Illinois: Multnomah Publishers, Inc., 1984.

Chapter 3

2. Moore, Beth. *Believing God*. Nashville, Tennessee: Broadman & Holman, 2004.

Chapter 4

3. *War Room*. Performance by Priscilla Shirer, directed by Alex Kendrick, Affirm Films, Kendrick Brothers Productions, Provident Films, 2015.

Chapter 5

4. Swindoll, Charles R. *The Grace Awakening*. Dallas, Texas: Word Publishing, 1990.

5. Stallings, John. "Learning to Lean." Benson Company, 1980.
6. Voskamp, Ann. *One Thousand Gifts*. Grand Rapids, Michigan: Zondervan, 2010.

Chapter 6

7. Fehr, Andrea. "Shock." *Divin' In*, August 21, 2013, https://calvinfehr.wordpress.com/2013/08/21/shock/
8. Waller, John. "While I'm Waiting." Crazy Faith. Reunion Records, 2009.
9. Tomlin, Chris. "With You." Hello Love. sixsteps, 2008.
10. Moore, Beth. *Believing God*. Nashville, Tennessee: Broadman & Holman, 2004.

Chapter 7

11. *NLT Dictionary/Concordance*. Carol Stream, Illinois: Tyndale House Publishers, 2007, p. 2406.
12. Shirer, Priscilla. *Fervent*. Nashville, Tennessee: B&H Publishing Group, 2015, p. 159.
13. Ibid., p. 161.

Chapter 8

14. Young, Sarah. *Jesus Calling*. Nashville, Tennessee: Thomas Nelson, 2004.
15. Fehr, Andrea. "Adventure." *Divin' In*, May 22, 2015, https://calvinfehr.wordpress.com/2015/05/22/the-adventure/
16. Williams, Kipp and Joshua David Silverberg and Jon White, Newsboys. "Live With Abandon." Restart, Sony/ATV Music Publishing LLC, Universal Music Publishing Group, 2013.
17. Redman, Beth and Matt. "Blessed Be the Name of the Lord." Capitol Christian Music Group, 2002.
18. Voskamp, Ann. *One Thousand Gifts*. Grand Rapids, Michigan: Zondervan, 2010.

19. Lane, Cristy. "One Day at a Time." One Day at a Time, LS Records 1981.

Chapter 9

20. Swindoll, Charles R. *The Grace Awakening*. Dallas, Texas: Word Publishing, 1990.
21. Fehr, Andrea. "Sacred Sitting." *Divin' In*, August 10, 2015, https://calvinfehr.wordpress.com/2015/08/10/sacred-sitting/
22. Montgomery, L. M. *Anne of Green Gables*. New York, New York: Bantam Books, 1987.
23. Talbot, John Michael and Steve Rabey. *The Lessons of St. Francis*. New York, New York: Penguin Group, 1998.
24. Ibid., p. 63.

Chapter 10

25. *The Simpsons*, produced by Matt Groenig and James L. Brooks, Fox, 1989 – present.
26. Fehr, Andrea. "Thud." *Divin' In*, June 2, 2013, https://calvinfehr.wordpress.com/2013/07/02/thud/
27. Meyer, Joyce. *21 Ways to Peace and Happiness*. Nashville, Tennessee: Faith Words, 2007.
28. Fehr, Andrea. "Busted." *Divin' In*, March 2, 2017, https://calvinfehr.wordpress.com/2017/03/02/busted/
29. Lewis, C. S. "The Screwtape Letters." *The Complete C.S. Lewis Signature Classics*. New York, New York: Harper One, 2007, p. 227.
30. Elliot, J. "Wherever You Are, Be All There." Author Academy Elite Webinar, 2018.
31. Young, Sarah. *Jesus Calling*. Nashville, Tennessee: Thomas Nelson, 2004.
32. Lewis, C. S. "The Screwtape Letters." *The Complete C.S. Lewis Signature Classics*. New York, New York: Harper One, 2007, p. 228.

Chapter 11

33. Brown, Brené. *Rising Strong.* New York, New York: Random House, 2017.

Chapter 13

34. Young, Sarah. *Jesus Calling.* Nashville, Tennessee: Thomas Nelson, 2004.
35. Henderson, Daniel. *Transforming Prayer.* Minneapolis, Minnesota: Bethany House Publishers, 2011.
36. Thomas, Gary. *Sacred Pathways.* Grand Rapids, Michigan: Zondervan, 2010, back cover.

Chapter 14

37. Brown, Brené. *Rising Strong.* New York, New York: Random House, 2017.

Chapter 16

38. Anderson, Tim and Alex Ebert and Filip Nikolic, Third Day. "The Victory." Miracle, Essential, 2012.
39. A.B. Simpson. "Happy All the Time." Brentwood- Benson Music Publishing, 1990.
40. Young, Sarah. *Jesus Calling.* Nashville, Tennessee: Thomas Nelson, 2004.
41. Young, WM. Paul. *Eve.* New York, New York: Howard Books, 2015, p. 42,43.

Other Resources

Grace Awakening by Charles R. Swindoll

Jesus Calling by Sarah Young

The Lessons of St. Francis by John Michael Talbot with Steve Rabey

Believing God Bible Study by Beth Moore through Living Proof Ministries

Get Out of That Pit by Beth Moore

21 Ways to Finding Peace and Happiness by Joyce Meyers

One Thousand Gifts by Ann Voskamp

Rising Strong by Dr. Brene Brown

Sacred Pathways by Gary Thomas

Fervent by Priscilla Shirer

Eve by WM. Paul Young

Acknowledgements

Highest thanks to my good God: You have faithfully sustained me and brought me across this finish line. Thank You for Your unending grace and patience with me. I will forever be grateful that you have equipped me to fly free. I love you, Abba.

To my ever-praying and supportive parents, Stan and Donna Porritt. I can't express my gratitude for your love and listening ears. I love you so very much, Momma and Daddy!

Momma, thank you for your excitement, encouragement, and for understanding the challenges faced by an author, speaker, and mom. Your gentle wisdom and practical advice have been so helpful.

Daddy, thank you for being the safe place for my first read-aloud. My heart was thrilled when you wanted to hear more. Thank you for your unconditional love and ability to bring calm perspective to new adventures.

To my wonderful in-laws, Ben and Pauline Fehr, who have cheered for me every step of the way.

To our treasures: I love you guys so much!

Thank you, Alaythea, for motivating me to move past my fear and publish.

Thank you, Benjamin, for all the hugs and empathy.

Thank you, Michael, for your curiosity and questions.

Thank you, Joshua, for your firm belief that I could finish this book.

Thank you all for brainstorming the title on the deck. Thank you for your blessing and encouragement to "go work on your book, Mom; it's your job."

To my hub, Calvin Fehr: You've always nudged me to do a bit more than I think I can, and you always stick around to help me do it. Thank you!!! Thank you for being there to hold me and pray or listen as I struggled along on this journey. Thank you for believing in me before I did. I'll love you forever.

To Caroline, Clint and Jen, Derek and Rye, Devin and Allie, Derek, Daniel, and Nick. I love you guys. You each inspire me as you continue to pursue the dreams that God has placed in your heart. I am so proud of each of you! Thank you for cheering for me!!!

To Ruthie and Craig Fehr: Thank you for modelling obedience to God no matter what and for your ongoing encouragement and love.

To my Dream Prayer Team: Just typing this makes my eyes well up with tears. Weekly, you guys have listened, loved, and prayed. Thank you!!! You'll never know how many times my heart was steadied because I knew you were behind me.

To Lori Heitrich, I love you, sister! You helped bring healing to my heart and hope to my soul. You introduced me to Kary Oberbrunner and Author Academy Elite. You have journeyed with me throughout this whole process and I am so very grateful for you! How great is our God!

To Alan Goff, my life coach, for teaching me what I would need so that I could accomplish my goal.

To Kary Oberbrunner my coach and publisher, thank you for always having my back and for believing in me before I believed in myself. Thank you for your AAE crew and program that led me through this whole process with grace, encouragement, wisdom and sucess. I'll always be thankful that you and David Branderhorst obeyed God and created Author Academy Elite and helped make my dreams come true.

Thank you also to Tracy for the amazing book cover.

Igniting Souls Tribe: You guys ROCK!!!!! Thank you for cheering me on continually, befriending and supporting me with your encouragement, honesty and inspirational action. I love you guys!!

Thank you for your sound advice, technology know –how and ongoing encouragement: Amy Martienz, Brenda Haire.

Thank you for editing magic and inspiration: Jill Gayoway, Lori Heitrich, Shannon McGann.

Thank you so very much for your willingness, time, diligence and encouragement while proofreading: Pat Massey, Lori Heitrich, Jennifer Porritt, Jill Gayoway, Jennifer Bergen. And a special thanks to those who were willing to be proofreaders.

To my Endorsers: Your endorsements continue to encourage me. Thank you: Kimberly Talmey, Gwen Hagerman, Kendra Madsen, Lori Heitrich, Brenda Haire, Victoria Lindahl, Alan Goff, Lyndon Wall. I respect each of you so very much for who you are and how you instill hope in those you encounter. It is my dream that one day I will have collaborated with each of you in empowering others to know and enjoy all that God has provided for us. Thank you so much for all you have done for me.

To my three Musketeers, Sarah Ibbotson, Lois Boersma, Ruth Schell: I love you!!! You guys believed in me before I did! Thank you for all the prayers and truth talks.

To the valiant women of Clairmont Community Church: You ladies are amazing!!! Your love and prayers are SUCH a gift to me. I'll be eternally grateful for you.

For powerful prayers and love: Andrea Corpas, Andrea Bergen, Amy Martienz, Uncle Ron and Aunt Judy Liddle, Grandma Lindahl, Brenda Haire, Cheree Quantz, Jenn Bergen, Sylvia Aspin, Cheryl Ikenouye, Rhonda Maki, Jill Gayoway, Jennifer Bergen, Rebecca Klassen, Tatiana Head, Sherri Bueckert.

You each have a special place in my heart. Thank you for bringing me back to Him time and time again! You are such gifts to me!

To anyone who has looked for their name but not seen it, I'm sorry. Thank you for your love and support.

To my very first coaching group: You guys are such a tremendous gift to me!!! The way God used you to confirm the message of *Freaking Out to Flying Free* continues to be inspirational for me. Thank you!!!

To you, my reader. I am thankful for you and proud of your desire to daily live out freedom. Thank you for reading my book and for sharing its message with others.

May God bless each of you abundantly just as you have blessed me!

About the Author

Hi there, my name is Andrea Fehr. I am a fun-loving and passionate follower of Jesus.

I have wrestled with depression, chronic illness and grief, and through these trials, I have discovered that my God is my everyday Savior, able to supply me with freedom and hope no matter what I am facing. I am a wife and a mother to four, a life coach, keynote speaker, author, and founder of Flying Free Ministries.

Contact me at: www.andreafehr.com

The purpose of Flying Free Ministries is to empower individuals to daily live out the freedom our everyday Savior provides. The resources provided at Flying Free Ministries are freedom-focus specific so that individuals can select tools that will specifically benefit them in their season of life.

Check out our resources at www.andreafehr.com.

CPSIA information can be obtained
at www.ICGtesting.com
Printed in the USA
LVHW03s2134101018
593145LV00014B/49/P